UNIVERSITY OF
GLOUCESTERSHIRE
CHELTENHAM *and* GLOUCESTER

Parochial Visi

Parochial Vision

The Future of the English Parish

Nick Spencer

PATERNOSTER

First published in 2004 by Paternoster Press

10 09 08 07 06 05 04   7 6 5 4 3 2 1

Paternoster Press is an imprint of Authentic Media,
PO Box 300, Carlisle, Cumbria CA3 0QS, UK
Box 1047, Waynesboro, GA 30830-2047, USA
www.paternoster-publishing.com

British Library Cataloguing in Publication Data

A catalogue record for this book is available from the British
Library

ISBN 1-84227-238-1

Cover Design by 4-9-0 ltd
Print Management by Adare Carwin
Printed and Bound in Denmark by Nørhaven Paperback

Dedication

Dedicated, with my love and thanks, to my parents, Howard and Christina.

Contents

Acknowledgements

I owe a great debt gratitude to those people who have helped me with the research and writing of *Parochial Vision*.

Peter Brierley and Christian Research provided the first vehicle for the idea, nearly four years ago, and Peter also took the time to share with me his considerable knowledge of the current state of the English church.

Professor Robin Gill kindly allowed me to see an advance copy of *The Empty Church Revisited*, which proved very useful, and also commented on a draft.

Hugh Cross, Bob Jackson, Gill Brentford, George Lings, Richard Hill, and Chris Neale all kindly volunteered time and information which helped shape my thinking, as did Simon Franklin, who did most to shake me from my subconsciously suburban perspective.

To Professor James Campbell, I owe gratitude both for his expert comments on the historical chapters of the manuscript and also for a most engaging introduction to the Anglo-Saxon world, over a decade ago.

I also owe a huge debt of thanks to Toby Hole, who tirelessly read through draft after draft, constantly providing a much-needed fresh perspective on the content and construction of the book, and to Kate, my wife, for her love and support for which I have no suitable words.

It should go without saying that all factual errors, naïve assumptions and poor jokes are mine alone.

Nick Spencer
London, 2003

Introduction

The Petrified Church

When Nick Leeson ruined Barings Bank in 1995 much was made of the fact that it was the oldest investment bank in the City of London. Founded in 1763 it had managed to flourish for nearly a quarter of a millennium before one over-enthusiastic trader brought it to its knees. Its heritage made it quintessentially English. The tragedy seemed all the greater because the bank was so old.

It was the same story when the Conservative government proposed closing St Batholomew's Hospital in the 1980s. The hospital dated back to the twelfth century but this meant nothing to a decade of creeping modernisation. There was a public outcry but much of the moral outrage managed to confuse building with institution. St Bart's may indeed have been founded in 1123 but it was no longer a religious organisation. It was not staffed by monks and did not offer shelter for pilgrims. It had been some years since Mass was held for healing the infirm. The location may not have changed in 900 years but everything else had.

In much the same way, Barings Bank may have been one of the most ancient and illustrious of the City of London's great institutions, and it may have been based on the same site since 1805, but it had long outgrown its first office – a Georgian house, with gardens at the back and stables to one side. Had it not done so, it is doubtful whether it would have survived the nineteenth century, let alone most of the twentieth.

One only has to look at the dictionary definition of the word church to see how Christianity in England has fared in this eternal struggle between institution and building: 'A building and extended uses . . . a building for public Christian worship . . . a temple . . .'. As the publication of countless books on English churches makes very clear, the Church of England is made of stone. Having started life as being founded on the Rock, it has become one.

This might be depressing were it not for the fact that those who are most acutely aware of it are Christians. It is the non-Christian public who are more likely to associate church with building, to lambast Victorians as church desecrators rather than church builders, and to become indignant about the abandonment of our national heritage when country churches are found locked on a Sunday.

Increasingly, Christians in England are recognising that church is a verb rather than a noun. It is something you do (and keep on doing) rather than something you are (and just live with). In truth, this realisation is at least as due to plummeting church attendance, as it is any new theological enterprise but that hardly constitutes a reason for criticism. Whatever the stimulus, fruit is being born slowly in all parts of the country, benefiting from a society that is no longer sure quite what community and belonging actually mean.

This book is a contribution to that movement. It looks at the parish system that has dominated the English landscape for a thousand years and proposes a new approach based on the system out of which parish churches grew. It is an open secret that many parish churches are in crisis, with rural vicars tiring themselves rushing between five or six parishes on a Sunday, and the energies and efforts of many parishioners exhausted on fund-raising events for leaking roofs. If for no other reason, the parish system needs to adapt to address this.

There are, however, many other good reasons for change. The last hundred years have seen English society alter beyond all recognition. People live, move, work, communicate, and relax in ways very different to their grandparents. If church is something people do rather than somewhere they go, it needs to take account of the lifestyles of these doers.

This is a proposition that often terrifies traditionalists who have visions of Sunday worship being sacrificed to the joys of Homebase, with the Church squeezing itself into the niche in people's lives left by consumerism. But adaptation need not be abandonment. Unless the Church of England willingly sacrifices the wrong things, it may end up unwillingly sacrificing the right ones.

As a contribution to 're-churching' England, it is easier to say what this book is not before explaining what it is. First and foremost, it is not a proposition for a branch closure programme. I do not suggest that the Church of England should abandon all parish churches with a congregation of under a dozen, pull out of all communities of less than 100 people, regroup in populous suburbs and start all over again. Such a strategy would be quite wrong, for all sorts of reasons that will become apparent. I have no pretensions or desire to be an ecclesiastical Dr Beeching.

Nor is it a Trojan horse used to smuggle a worship band into the choir stalls. Some current thinking sadly views modern church as synonymous with modern worship styles. People who see a drum kit as the only way that a church can identify with modern culture are as guilty of setting up idols as those who deem anything post-Authorised Version as against the will of God. The cross is the salvation of humankind, not the electric guitar.

Nor, finally, is the book an updated *Faith in the Countryside*. Its focus is at once much narrower and much broader: narrower in that it makes no attempt to cover the range of issues examined in that report, such as the economy in rural areas or the environment and rural development, and broader in that it has as much an interest in urban and suburban faith practice as it does in rural.

It differs from *Faith in the Countryside* in one other important respect. That publication was an official report by a committee of over twenty experts from different fields. This book is nothing of the kind, comprising the fruit of one person's research and thinking, written from a personal point of view and intended to be an interesting read just as much as a serious proposition.

What, then, is this serious proposition? The book is divided into seven chapters. The first two survey the rise and fall of the English parish system, covering its haphazard evolution at the end of the Anglo-Saxon period, its fluid development in the Middle Ages, its response to reformation, restoration and revolution, and its gradual decline in the nineteenth and twentieth centuries. The section makes no pretence at being a comprehensive history of the English parish. Longer and more detailed volumes have been published in recent years that do that admirably. Instead, the intention is to trace one strand of thought through a thousand years of demographic, social and cultural history: that the parish system was not brought down from Mount Sinai pure and divinely inspired, but evolved and adapted to suit the needs of English worshippers. In spite of what many non-Christians think, the parish is not set in stone.

The third chapter returns to the first millennium. It looks at how the parish system evolved from a pre-existing church structure comprising of collegiate, 'minster' churches, with large 'parochiae', peripatetic clergy, relative local autonomy and an evangelistic outlook. This is not merely an interesting historical detail but central to the entire book. It is a peculiarity of English society today that, in many important ways, the twenty-first century has more in common with the seventh and eighth than it does with any intervening ones. The minster church is not only more primitive than the parish, satisfying that seemingly unquenchable English desire for historical authenticity, but actually more appropriate to our needs today. We need to go back for the future.

Chapter four looks in greater detail at contemporary British society. Rather than attempting the impossible, comprehensive 'state of the nation' in 8,000 words, it focuses on a handful of major social trends that all point past the current parochial model and calls for a new approach to structuring the Church of England. The following chapter moves on to a smaller number of ecclesiastical trends, each of which demand a new way of thinking about parishes. Throughout both chapters, the minster model is commended as a way of addressing problems and facing the future with confidence.

Chapter six proceeds to make what, to my mind, is the most convincing case for a return to minster churches. Put simply, we are heading in that direction anyway. Throughout the twentieth century, a number of Church reports and prescient individual opinions expressed the need for the English parish structure to change, and many pointed towards the ideas expressed in this book. The most recent have even, to my shock, used the terminology of minster churches. Even more pointedly, church attendance patterns suggest that an ad hoc minster system already exists in England today. We are simply following where we are being led.

The final chapter offers some proposals as to precisely where that may be. It is one thing writing about the future of the English parish and examining theoretical models for its development. It is quite another actually implementing them. The book, therefore, concludes with some *tentative* suggestions as to how the future might take shape. As will be seen, they are anything but definitive or prescriptive. One of the key characteristics of the minster model is the openness to local variation and autonomy. It eschews a one-size-fits-all approach. The ideas outlined may be adopted, adapted or ignored as local circumstances see fit.

There are two, perhaps striking omissions in the book: an overt theological analysis and a detailed discussion of ecumenism. Although both have informed the book's thinking, I have avoided any explicit engagement with them. Whatever parochial restructuring the Church of England does engage in during the twenty-first century, it must be underpinned by a careful theological analysis of the motivations and the desire to foster ecumenical links wherever possible.

Nevertheless, for the purposes of this book the merits of simplicity were deemed to outweigh those of comprehensiveness. Perhaps more importantly, the historical, sociological and ecclesiastical angles from which the English parish is surveyed, have, in truth, proved considerably more important than theological or ecumenical ones in shaping the parochial system as it is today. To assess the future of the English parish, it is imperative to have a realistic view of what it actually is!

The final and ultimately critical point to make is that the future of the Church of England rests in the hands of the faithful. If it is to survive the coming years, let alone grow, it will be due to the efforts of men and women across the country, working with God and with each other, making tiny differences on a daily basis that are too small to be measured on any human scale, but vast when seen against the big picture. I can only hope that the ideas and suggestions in this book might stimulate such men and women to influence their immediate environment in some small, important way.

1

The Rise and Fall of the English Parish

Politics and Religion

The Bible is not often quoted on television. Occasionally the odd phrase from the Authorised Version will creep in. We hear of swords being beaten into ploughshares, of thorns in the flesh and of powers that be, but in reality these maxims have long since passed into our national bloodstream and are about as religious as the Shakespearean proverbs or Wildean witticisms that grace our screens with similar frequency.

There is one exception, however. It is a scene that is rehearsed on current affairs programmes with such peculiar regularity that it sounds almost scripted. The Church has published a report on inner city poverty or the treatment of asylum seekers or some such issue and the 'Bishop of Somewhere' has been called up to explain and defend the conclusions. Questions are addressed and answers offered. Accusations are levelled and refuted. And then, about three-quarters of the way into the interview, the interviewer will almost invariably say something like, 'There is a wider question here, isn't there?

Should the Church really be getting involved in politics in this way? I mean, aren't you in danger of mixing up the things of God with the things of Caesar?'

There it is – the Gospel according to St Matthew, chapter 22, verse 21 – hacked out of context and shoved under the studio spotlight. The Temple is nowhere to be seen. The Pharisees and the Herodians have disappeared and Jesus himself is only lurking vaguely in the background. 'Render unto Caesar the things which are Caesar's; and unto God the things which are God's.'

The question is almost comic in its misconception. The assumptions beneath the interviewer's inquiry are delightfully naïve, based as they are on a king who is not interested in his subject's dearest and deepest loyalties, and a God who generously agrees to withdraw from all political arenas and mind his own business with 'churchy' things.

The reality is somewhat different and more muddled. The division between politics and religion is a purely modern invention that would have made no sense to Jesus or his contemporaries. Twenty-first-century Britain is very different to first-century Palestine, but the tradition of infecting politics with quarrelsome religion is, thankfully, still going strong.

This is a source of huge frustration to some commentators who would prefer religion to crawl back under a rock where they can criticise it for being too parochial and self-interested. Such an attitude has led to the popular idea that secular ties automatically invalidate religious conviction. If it has something to do with earth, it can have nothing to do with heaven.

This is, however, nonsense. As has been observed on innumerable occasions, Christianity is an earthly religion concerned with life *before* death just as much as life *after* it. Christians' belief about the latter has long shaped their attitude to the former, often compelling an involvement in 'politics'. The modern separation of politics and religion, feeding, as it does, on Reformation wrangles between faith and works, misses the point altogether. Every public act is, ultimately, somehow political. It just so happens that those acts of the Established Church are more obviously so.

The Church in England has been involved in English 'politics' from day one. When Augustine landed in Kent in 597 AD, he was welcomed by a king whose wife was already a Christian. Bertha, a Frankish princess, had brought a priest with her when she moved to Kent to marry King Ethelbert. He, in return, repaired a church for her in Canterbury, where she might worship. Even before the English were Christians, the English Church was 'political'.

A great deal changed over the subsequent centuries but this principle remained secure. In 1953, Queen Elizabeth II was crowned monarch in a ceremony which could be traced back nearly a thousand years to when King Edgar was crowned in Bath in 973. Her title of Defender of the Faith was inherited from Henry VIII, who was granted it by a grateful Pope Leo X in 1521. There are currently twenty-six bishops sitting in the House of Lords, a tradition dating back to the Middle Ages, and every day the business of the House of Commons is opened with prayer. Whether you like it or not, for much of the last 1,500 years, it has been fiendishly difficult to separate the things of Caesar from the things of God.

This is the key to understanding the English parish. The parish system grew out of this soil of confused loyalties, maturing through a messy mix of faith and expediency, spiritual ideals and earthly ambitions. But its intricate involvement with worldly powers did not render it anathema to true religion; if anything it did the opposite. Our judgements to the contrary show us to be anachronistic, naïve or both.

The Perfect Business Strategy

We owe a great debt to Simon Jenkins. His popular book *England's Thousand Best Churches*, published in 1999, did what no previous guide had quite had the courage to do and give the chosen sites a five-star ranking system:

> One and two stars indicate churches worth visiting for just a few features, and these are bound to be rather arbitrary. Three stars and above should embrace all the outstanding (and open) parish churches in England. The top hundred, with four of five stars, either demand a long visit or include works that would feature in the entrance hall of my 'virtual' museum.[1]

We are under no illusions here. This is Michelin Guide territory and what we are surveying is more important than food or even church architecture. This is not simply another kind of cultural guide or a prototype 'Rough Guide to Spiritual England'. As Jenkins says, parish churches are essentially a guide *to ourselves*, a mirror held up to our own identity:

> I see my churches as witness to the bonds that have brought the English people together in village and town through a thousand years of history. They are memory in stone … It is through the churches of England that we learn who we were and thus who we are and might become.[2]

Jenkins is certainly right in suggesting that the English parish and its church comprise something more than ecclesiastical art and architecture. They are, indeed, a palimpsest of our social and cultural history, with all the compromise and confusion that entailed. Above all, they are the intersection of religious life with secular power and have been so for as long as we can see. The first years of the English parish system are difficult to discern, with evidence before the 1200s being very piece-meal, but as far as it is possible to tell, it appears that the local village church was the brainchild not of theologians or archbishops but of local 'secular' lords.

Writing in the 730s, the historian Bede tells how, around 670, the archbishop of York was called upon to consecrate the churches of two thegns, or low-ranking nobles, Puch and Addi. Today, a single small church dating from that period still stands at Escomb in County Durham. These small, local churches appear to have been anomalies in an age when the Church favoured larger, minster churches. It is clear, at least, that the two churches mentioned by Bede were 'patronal': they were set-up, funded and effectively owned by local lords. When, several hundred years later, such churches began to appear across England, this was the model on which they were run.

Parishes were formed as larger areas of land, such as royal estates, were broken up. The lords and thegns who owned the resulting estates often founded churches on them, sometimes gaining consent from the local minster church but more often not, thus causing confusion and arguments over following years. The fact is that the founding of local churches was often conducted with the minimum of ecclesiastical involvement. Parish churches had, at first, very little to do with the Church.

There were three driving reasons behind the evolution of the parish church. First and most importantly, money; secondly, social prestige; and thirdly, pastoral work and the cure of souls.

It is rather appropriate that the first lists of churches in England were made for tax purposes. These date from several hundred years after the emergence of the parish network but point towards its foundational feature. As a way of making money, the parish church was almost foolproof.

Every Christian owed an obligation to his or her church. Such payments were enjoined in Scripture and reinforced and expanded in canon law. They extended beyond the famous tithe to include church-scot, soul-scot, plough-alms and hearth-penny. Early Saxon laws made it clear that obligations were owed to the minster church but with the break-up of the minsters' own parishes or 'parochiae', such payments were frequently diverted to the local church. By founding a church on his manor, a thegn could appropriate a significant income stream that was compulsory and resolutely imposed. Royal enforcement of tithe probably underpinned the development of the entire English parish system.

The thegn would, in return, have to staff his church and hence the local priest would essentially be his lord's man, answerable to him rather than the distant bishop with whom he would have minimal contact. His duties were primarily liturgical, praying, observing festivals, singing hours, celebrating Mass and baptising infants. He would also have some pastoral and didactic duties, such as ministering to the sick, teaching the Lord's Prayer and creeds, and expounding the gospel.

This was the theory. In reality, although evidence is scarce, it appears that priests were hardly different from their flock, being poor, labouring and hardly educated. Many of them were married (and might have a concubine) and would often bequeath the church to one of their sons. Various laws cautioned priests against drunkenness, singing in taverns, carrying weapons and fighting one another. An incident from the *Life of Saint Wulfstan*, the Bishop of Worcester, suggests that some priests were as money-driven as their lords: 'priests refused to administer that sacrament to infants unless the parents would fill their pockets'.[3]

Parish churches were the boom industry at the turn of the first millennium. Around the tenth century they began to appear like 'mushrooms in the night'. Thegns realised that by setting one up they were effectively founding a mint on their land. It was for this reason that the churchman Aelfric complained that men bartered and traded churches in the same way they did mills. Parish churches were a lucrative business.

The second reason, closely linked to these fiscal benefits, was the implication a parish church had for social prestige. Churches were privately owned. They belonged first and foremost to the local lord rather than his people. Just as larger territories had accommodated minster churches or corresponded to dioceses, so smaller manors deserved their ecclesiastical equivalent. The ownership of a church was a status symbol. To have a church was to show that you were a long way up the social ladder. Parish churches became, alongside other symbols such as 'a seat at the king's table' or 'a protected homestead', a means of showing that you had arrived.

The third reason, which should be not be downplayed, is the one we would consider to be more acceptable: pastoral work and the need for fellowship. These had been central to the formation of minster churches many centuries beforehand and so when these churches broke up and became (in some cases) parish churches themselves, and when their field churches were elevated to parochial status, the new, smaller churches adapted a pastoral role.

In case it needs stating again, this hotchpotch, self-interested, pastorally concerned, economically minded evolution does not automatically invalidate the parish system. We should not judge what *is* according solely to what *was*. Much changed over the next thousand years and it is, in any case, quite wrong to impose modern categories on a medieval system. The parish system would not have lasted ten centuries, albeit with frequent modifications, had it not satisfied the needs of the men and women who built, maintained and attended its churches. It does, however, suggest that, at least in origin, the English parish was frequently an accidental, secular, malleable creature whose strength came not from its brilliant strategic thinking or divine inspiration but from its capacity to reform itself around the needs of its lords, priests and parishioners.

Counting Sheep Pens

The exact number of parishes in Britain has never really been known. The haphazard and individualised manner of their creation meant that there was never any record of when and how many were created. The Domesday Book is a poor guide to the number of churches in the country, providing the relevant evidence for only a number of counties and giving no real idea how the number of manors related to the number of churches. In the total area surveyed, including places where only a priest is named, there is evidence for fewer than 2,300 churches (out of over 13,000 place names). There is no doubt that this is a fractional record, with many other churches being included in the valuation of the manor.

While we do not know the number of parishes that came under William's control in 1066, evidence suggests that the century following the Norman Conquest witnessed a significant building programme. There are a large number of churches today whose oldest fabric dates from the twelfth century. Many of these new stone churches may have been refoundations built on the sites of smaller wooden churches, whose only survivor is at Greensted in Essex. Nevertheless, we have every reason to think that the framework for today's parish network was in place by the mid-twelfth century.

It is from this time that the first church lists date. The *Valuation of Norwich* and the *Taxatio* of Pope Nicholas IV date from 1254 and 1291, respectively, and were compiled for the purposes of raising taxes for a crusade. Given the economic origins of so many parish churches it seems only fitting that our first church lists were created for financial reasons. The *Taxatio* of Pope Nicholas IV records just over 8,000 parishes in England, a number that almost certainly excludes a number of churches that were too poor to pay the papal tax.

Some 250 years later Henry VIII ordered a more detailed list of churches, in anticipation of his great land seizure. This document, the *Valor Ecclesiasticus*, records slightly over 8,800 churches, a 10 per cent rise on the earlier list. The parish system, once established, seems to have changed remarkably little over quarter of a millennium.

This tiny rise in the number of parish churches appears to have slowed even further over the sixteenth and seventeenth centuries. An abortive attempt by the Commonwealth to reorganise the whole parish structure made little difference. Thomas Wilson, in his essay, *The State of England 1600*,[4] suggested a figure of 9,725 churches in England and Wales and nearly a century later Gregory King estimated that there were 10,000 clergy holding glebes. There was a slight increase in the eighteenth century so that in the early national censuses approximately 11,000 parish registers were recorded. Victoria's reign would change all this but, at least superficially, the English parish had remained a remarkably constant entity for over 600 years. The overall figures, however, mask considerable variety on the ground.

The Rural Parish and Beyond

John Rickman, who compiled reports on the first four censuses in the nineteenth century, wrote in his 'Preliminary Observations' in the 1821 census, 'The Question What is a parish? has often occurred, and has been found not easily determinable.' His question was largely due to the growing industrialisation and urbanisation of the time but might well have been asked in the Middle Ages.

Parish churches

In rural areas alone there were five discernible types of church. The first and largest group was that of churches whose parochial status was unquestioned. Their rectors received tithes and oblations. They had cemeteries and baptismal fonts, and the bishop instituted their priests. They had cure of souls and were authorised to perform the usual sacraments.

However, even this group was malleable according to circumstances. Although remarkably few 'official' churches were ever completely abandoned, parishes and their churches were often merged when parishioners became unable to support their own church. Although one might have expected an increase in parishes and churches during the years of rising population in the early fourteenth century, this was also a period of poverty and strain on resources and there appears to have been a lull in building. Conversely, the great population decline of the late fourteenth century, which accounted for many of the 3,000 known abandoned settlements in England appears to have heralded a great period of church building. The parish church was an unpredictable beast.

Changes very much depended on individual parish management and this was often whimsical. The first parishes accorded to local manors and the first parish churches were essentially private chapels. There followed in the eleventh and twelfth centuries a period of reform in the Western Church in which the Church freed itself from secular power at all levels. This became known as the period of appropriation, when the Church set its face against the control that lay patrons exercised over the appointment of priests and the incomes of their patronal churches. Defects in the system were targeted. Unsuitable men, including those who were married or treated their position as hereditary, were evicted. Patrons who used their church primarily as a convenient family perquisite were pursued. The practice of simony, the commercial exchange and partitioning of benefices, the treatment of a benefice as simply a profitable adjunct to a manor were all customs determinedly reformed.

In seeking to wrest this power from secular lords, the Church marketed salvation. Monasteries grew as the laity were encouraged to atone for their lives by giving donations to institutions which would pray for them or assure them of salvation. In this new marketplace, land was the most prized gift, but not far behind it was the benefice of a church. As the Middle Ages progressed, more parish churches came under the management of a local (or not so local) monastery.

In this way, the Church claimed the 'advowson' or right to nominate the parish priest from the local lay lord, strengthening its presence across the land. More importantly, it acquired several sources of income, supreme among which was the tithe. Just as setting up local parish churches had been the early medieval equivalent of a business venture, so the age of appropriation was that of the business takeover. As the historian, Nicholas Pounds has said:

> Tithe was the cement which bound the parish together … it was the tithe which the patrons of livings most often clung to, and it was tithe – not theoretical considerations of the superiority of divine law over human, of canon over secular – that led monasteries to appropriate benefices in their hundreds.[5]

The Church was so successful in inculcating canon law doctrine that evasion of tithe became a mortal sin and resistance was minimal for centuries and unquestioned until John Selden's *History of Tithes* (1618), although disputes over exactly what was tithable were legion.

The process of appropriation went on throughout the Middle Ages. By the time of the Reformation, England's 9,000 or so parish churches were under a wide variety of owners. Each would have been deeply concerned with economics but motives and interests differed according to patrons, and this variety of internal structure, accompanied with the broader demographic and economic changes across regions meant that although the system of definite parishes in England was well and surely established, there was a significant degree of variety within the overall homogeneity.

Chapels of ease

Below the level of established parishes were chapels of ease or chapelries. These rarely received any part of the tithe and they tended not to possess either baptismal fonts or rights of burial. Those who lived within their limits, with some exceptions in the north, had their children baptised and were buried at the parish or mother church. Towards the end of the Middle Ages some chapelries succeeded in obtaining baptismal and burial rights.

Parishioners who were too far away from the parish church set up chapels. Unlike parish churches they tended to be grass-roots establishments. Only rarely did these chapelgoers receive an income from the parochial church. Instead, they had to rely on their own funds to construct and maintain the building and support the chaplain. Moreover, those parishioners that did fund a chapel were rarely exempt from their duties to their parish church.

In this way, chapels were truly communal ventures, indicating a degree of initiative, determination and social cohesion that appears, at least superficially, to be less important at the parish level. But chapelgoers also had to bear considerable financial strain, with little if any institutional support, and so chapels were often short-lived or exceedingly poor institutions. No one knows how many chapels were founded, used and dismantled or abandoned in the Middle Ages but it is likely to be in the thousands. Their permanence depended on the area and parish in which they were founded and in larger parishes, especially in northern counties, there would have been many.

Some chapels eventually seceded from their parishes and became parish churches themselves, although the income implications this had for the parochial church made it an infrequent, resisted and unpopular move. In Yorkshire and Lancashire, the counties with, on average, the largest parishes, a system of quasi-parishes developed serving the spiritual needs of inhabitants of the many small settlements which were a long way away from their parochial church.

In medieval chapels we see an organic movement that was to become more familiar with the spread of non-conformism centuries later. The crucial difference between them was that chapels, no matter what the particular circumstances were, had to operate within the pre-existing parochial structure, whereas nonconformists were operating wholly and purposefully outside it.

Oratories

At the third level down were private chapels or oratories. These were founded in castles, private homes, rectories, hospitals and guildhalls. The underlying motive for their development was escapism. Lords and ladies who did not wish to mix with labourers and peasants established their own places of worship that were not open to the general public. Official reasons tended, naturally, to be more circumspect, with lordly requests often using the same reasons as the laity did for chapels, such as the distance to the parish church, the hazardousness of the journey or infirmity of travellers. Their use was usually restricted by ecclesiastical edict to the family that had established them or at most the family's community and it was their responsibility to maintain them.

By the thirteenth century most baronial castles had a chapel and this trend spread downwards, with licensing becoming increasingly lax. Oratories are another example of variation upon a theme; individual needs created a different structure that operated, sometimes uneasily, within the overall parish structure.

Chantries

Yet another group was that of chantries. The sole purpose of these institutions was the celebration of mass for the repose of the souls of their founders and of other carefully specified groups. They grew in popularity as the doctrine of purgatory gained ground in the later Middle Ages. Between 1281 and 1534 licences for over 2,000 chantries were granted.

As with chapels, their existence was contingent on the funding of a specified group or family, and they disappeared with far greater regularity than parish churches. Although a number appear to have been dismantled in advance, their final demise came with the dissolution in the 1530s.

Wayside chapels

The final idiosyncratic group was that of the chapels that existed on bridges and on roadsides, the most famous of which was the chapel to Thomas Beckett on London Bridge. The ownership and precise purpose of these is rarely known today but logic suggests they existed for the spiritual comfort of travellers. Their very position meant that they had no parishioners as such. They were the medieval equivalent of airport chapels.

Conclusion

These various ecclesiastical buildings, together with their particular jurisdictions, made the ecclesiastical landscape of England rather more complex than a monolithically parish-church based picture would have us believe. Nicholas Pounds writes: 'all these categories overlapped, and each encroached on the functions of the others. It was impossible to draw a line between them.'[6] The ecclesiastical structure in rural areas in the Middle Ages was a spectrum, with the lower, smaller end being particularly fluid, with some chapels and oratories disappearing with little trace and others obtaining baptismal rights and becoming parishes in their own right. The arrangement was even more fluid in towns.

Parishes and Towns

When Pope Gregory sent Augustine to the English at the end of the sixth century, he did so with the plan of establishing a diocesan pattern based on the geography of Roman Britain: there were to be two archdioceses headed up from London and York, each supervising twelve dioceses based in other towns. The reality turned out somewhat differently.

The intervening centuries had taken a heavy toll on Roman Britain and by the time Augustine arrived all towns were in a state of advanced decay. When Christianity finally spread through the island in the seventh century, it did so as a rural religion. Some towns grew up around churches but it was not until the final centuries of the Saxon era that any became large enough to demand a parish structure of their own. On the eve of the Norman Conquest, a small number – including London, Norwich, Lincoln and York – had upwards of fifty churches each.

The great period of urban foundation came after the Conquest, however, with both towns and the urban parishes within them proliferating in the twelfth and thirteenth centuries. Although this was also the great period of rural church building, there were a number of differences between urban and rural parishes.

First, in medieval towns, while there were sokes (areas of local jurisdiction), there was no equivalent of a manorial patron. There was, therefore, no single person to found, endow, own and govern a church as there was in the countryside. Although many may have been family businesses, at least in the eleventh and twelfth centuries, and run by hereditary priests, the urban parish tended not to be a business venture in the same way as its rural counterpart.

Secondly, towns were busier and more fluid environments than villages, with no obvious discrete areas for parishes to serve and, more importantly, no agricultural produce to tithe. Tithing did still exist but the inherent difficulty in recording, measuring and taking it made the whole prospect of urban parishes less financially enticing.

Thirdly, and most importantly, instead of the half-free ceorls (ordinary, non-noble freemen) who dominated rural villages, medieval towns were populated with freemen who could and did build and run churches according to their own needs. Urban parishes were, by and large, created 'from below'; they developed from communal enterprises and belonged to the community in a way that few rural parishes did. On the occasions when ordinary people owned a church in a rural area they would be described as *liberi homines* or freemen; although this was not uncommon in the Danelaw of eastern England, it was the exception elsewhere.

Urban parishes tended to be independent neighbourhood churches that were small and insubstantial (and poorly recorded), again growing from efforts of town dwellers, in much the same way as nonconformist chapels did 500 years later. They were founded through the determination of a small group of like-minded individuals, but prospered only when there was sufficient wealth and energy to sustain them.

For this reason, many early towns were heavily over-churched and there was much wastage throughout the Middle Ages. Winchester, for example, already waning as a major town, boasted seventy churches by the twelfth century, which amounted to virtually one on every street corner. This number declined steadily over the following centuries to reach twenty-six in the 1530s and twelve by 1600. When one compares this to the permanence of most rural parish churches, it is easy to see the precariousness and fluidity of parish structures in the medieval town. Only the most prosperous towns such as London and Norwich did not lose churches on any scale.

As one would expect given such an ad hoc system of foundation, urban parishes varied greatly, often within the same town. Most towns had one pre-eminent parish, bigger, more elaborate and with greater influence than the others. Some parishes would be twenty times larger than others in the same town. Many urban churches, the majority of which we have no records for, were tiny, temporary affairs more akin to meeting halls, and it was never really clear who owned, managed, sustained or officiated at them. Quite a number of urban parishes were too poor to be included in the thirteenth-century tax lists, which provide our first detailed record of English parishes.

Some sizeable towns never had more than a handful of parishes through the entire Middle Ages, whereas others like Winchester had scores and London, famously, had over one hundred. Town dwellers liked to found and abandon churches with relative impunity and were only prevented from doing so where there was an active and powerful local landlord, often a monastery, whose financial benefits were threatened by the proliferation. Less obviously and easily tithe-able as they were, urban churches could still provide profitable income streams and were still bought, sold and leased in same way as rural parishes.

Just as there was little to prevent the explosion of churches in many towns in the twelfth and thirteenth centuries, so there was little to stop the equally rapid decline in their number towards the end of the Middle Ages. Reasons for wastage were varied. A decline in population in the wake of the Black Death followed by a decline in urban prosperity in the fifteenth century were the major reasons but there were other contributing factors. Fashions in worship changed with people preferring more elaborate, 'professional' services at which the grander churches excelled. Similarly, the rich merchants and urban elite on whom so much urban church building depended increasingly put their money into churches which were already outstanding in terms of art and architecture rather than found new ones. Accordingly, a gulf opened up between a few grand churches and the rest. As the Middle Ages ended, the urban parish structure appeared to be becoming more stable.

To generalise about any half-millennial period is dangerous. The ecclesiastical landscape was very different during the reign of Ethelred the Unready from that under Henry VII. Nevertheless, if any single generalisation is justifiable it is that the parish structure, while dominating the English landscape for most of those 500 years was never a uniform, precisely structured and rigidly obeyed institution. Wherever there could be, there was a great deal of variation, the only inhibiting factor being the presence of vested (usually financial) interests.

When these were absent, as in certain towns, the parish structure would all but dissolve. It has been estimated that if you were to include cathedrals, monasteries, hospitals, chapels, chantries, oratories, wayside chapels and the buildings of the Templars and Hospitallers in your calculations, there were probably more non-parochial than parochial churches in medieval England.

Even where the structural and economic prohibitions were in place, as they were in most rural areas, there would be a great deal of adaptation and modification. Churches ascended and descended the ladder of hierarchy, parishes merged and split, and boundary disputes were legion. Within an overall structure, itself developed and perpetuated primarily for financial reasons, there was considerable variety and flexibility. It seemed that parishioners could do pretty much what they wanted as long as they played by certain basic rules.

Reformation, Revolution and Restoration

While the Reformation had an incalculable impact on thousands of English parish churches, it had very little effect on the English parish structure. In the space of a few years Mass was abolished, Mass books and breviaries were surrendered, altars drawn down, statues defaced, walls whitened and windows broken. The paraphernalia of late-medieval Christianity, veils, vestments, chalices, chests and hangings were surrendered to the King's commissioners. Clergy and parishioners were ordered to 'take away, utterly extinct and destroy all shrines, coverings of shrines, all tables, candlesticks, trundles, or rolls of wax, pictures, paintings and all other monuments of feigned miracles, pilgrimages, idolatry and superstition'.[7] Iconoclasm was a central aspect of the Edwardine reforms.

In their place, parishes received a succession of newly translated grand Bibles and centrally authorised prayer books. English parish churches changed beyond all recognition. Within a single generation, the practice of religion was overturned.

These changes in the daily ritual and detail of religious practice within local churches were not mirrored in the overall structure by which these local churches related to one another. There were fears that once the monasteries had been dissolved, the parishes, many of which were owned by monasteries, would follow but they proved to be unfounded. There was no attempt on the part of the reformers to destroy the structure they inherited. Indeed, they were keener to manage the existing system in such a way as allowed them to implement their theology than they were to replace it.

A small number of changes were made but they constituted no more than a tinkering at the edge of the system. In 1545 permission was granted to demolish a church building if it stood within a mile of another or if the inhabitants could not raise nine marks a year for the priest. Two years later, the second Chantries Act included a statement that it was not intended to close 'any chapel made or ordained for the ease of people dwelling distant from the parish church'.

To a degree, it was the parish structure that shaped the English Reformation rather than the English Reformation that shaped the parish structure. The extent of Reformation often differed according to the size of a parish, how rural it was, and how close it was to the source of new ideas. Smaller, more southern, eastern and, of course, more urban parishes tended to be more receptive to Reformation ideas, although this was not a cast-iron rule. Kendal in Cumbria became staunchly Protestant following the appointment of two Protestant vicars in 1551 and 1562.

Perhaps the biggest structural implication that the Reformation had on the parish system was with the dissolution of the monasteries. As monasteries were disbanded and sold off, the benefices they had appropriated over previous centuries were re-appropriated once more to laymen. Once again, parishes had a different owner and once again, after several hundred years, for many churches it was a secular lord. Subsequent visitation records suggest that the new 'lay' estates were even more grasping and less caring than previous monastic ones and that, in spite of the wholesale redesign work that accompanied the Reformation, church fabric in later Tudor years was in a shocking condition.

While the Reformation had little obvious impact on the system of English parishes, it did sow the seeds that would eventually lead to its destruction. First, it internalised religion. Pre-Reformation England was a supremely religious culture, with local custom, art and drama all impregnated with religious folkloric elements. The Reformation changed that utterly, denying the healing power of saints, the power of religious imagery, the importance of much ritual and the authority of the priest. Instead, there grew up a culture of reading and inward digestion, founded on the idea of a priesthood of all believers. Demonstration of faith became unnecessary or even suspect. The raison d'être of the late medieval parish, the necessary public incarnation of religious faith, was thus removed. The churches were still there, as was their legal jurisdiction, but their religious heart had been removed. It was replaced, to a large degree, by what one might call 'official business' as churches became closely tied to local government. Unlike their urban counterparts, which had always operated alongside existing organisational structures, such as wards or leets, rural parishes gradually assumed local government roles, particularly as the manor decayed.

Accordingly, the parish's civil responsibilities increased greatly at the Reformation. From 1536 parishes were asked to provide for the poor. From 1538 they kept records on baptisms, marriages and burials. From 1555 each parish was made responsible by an act of parliament for the repair of highways within its bounds, with local men working four, and later six, days a year on this task. A new group of parish officials was introduced: the surveyors of highways and, in 1572, overseers of poor were added to parishes' offices. Thirty years later the Elizabethan Poor Law gave real authority to overseers, chosen by ratepayers in cooperation with churchwardens to raise and spend money on poor relief. For the next 300 years the parish provided the basic framework of the nation's civil administration. There was, after all, no other national organisation with 9,000 branch offices. When Thomas Cromwell instructed each parish to keep a register of baptisms, marriages and burials, parishes effectively became local branch offices of the Tudor Office for National Statistics. The Church thus became a curious hybrid of administration, organisation and a peculiarly English religion. Parishes became the vessels of English history, detailing the birth and death of every person, and the bastions of the *via media* that Anglicanism represented. They have been valued for both ever since.

The Reformation also began the gradual atomisation of society. This is not to suggest that we can trace the origins of our modern individualised culture to William Tyndale or Thomas Cranmer, but rather to say that, after the Reformation, authority lost its power to unite a spectrum of differing beliefs. The Pope, arguably the greatest single figure of authority in Europe, had been dethroned, and although the monarch replaced him, the ideological basis for the king's supreme authority was less convincing. At a local level, the priest had been demystified. Lay literacy and autonomy were encouraged, although feared. The ideological cords that bound communities together had been slackened.

Following the Reformation there was no effective means of uniting the ever-widening spectrum of theological opinion. For parishes this meant that the overarching parochial system that had been maintained over the previous centuries, largely by being underpinned by absolute ecclesiastical authority, was fatally weakened. In the early post-Reformation years this had little or no effect. The real impact would not be seen for another 150 years, when it would critically decay this foundational institution. As soon as people could legally set up churches that had no affiliation to the national one, they did. The seeds of change had been sown.

The first cracks in the parish structure began to appear during the seventeenth century. The Act of Uniformity still held in the opening years of the century with no new places of worship being permitted outside the Anglican Church, but all this changed with the outbreak of the Civil War.

The Puritans were generally tolerant towards divergent groups or conventicles but had little time for the Established Church and during the Commonwealth they set about dismantling it. The territorial offices of the Church – such as archbishop, bishop and archdeacon – were abolished and church courts were suppressed. In their place, the Puritan government tried to establish a Presbyterian type of church government, as existed in Scotland.

Only in Lancashire was reorganisation in any way successful. Parishes were retained but were grouped into *classes*, each consisting of a group of neighbouring parishes and bearing a close similarity to the hundred and to rural deaneries. These *classes* assumed many of the functions that had previously been discharged by the archdeacon's visitations, which had themselves been organised on the basis of rural deaneries.

One 1650 survey and report of Lancashire went further and suggested changing the parish structure altogether. It recommended upgrading many chapels to parochial status, building a number of new churches, transferring townships from one parish to another, and limiting new parochial boundaries in the light of the distances that some parishioners had to travel. The scheme came to nothing.

As with the Reformation, the longer-term effects of the Civil War and the Commonwealth were subtler. The Interregnum did much to damage the folk culture of parish life that had survived the Reformation. Puritan zeal attacked festivities such as church-ales, maypole dances and other seasonal celebrations, and although many traditions were revived at the Restoration, the impetus had been lost and customs died. Revivals in the nineteenth century were more determined but even less authentic than those of the Restoration period, predicated as they were on an anachronistic understanding of medieval society, and leaving us with many of the kitsch and stereotyped olde-English customs we know and love today.

Administratively, the Anglican parish remained as intact and as important in 1660 as it had been half a century before, but it was no longer as integral to community life as it had been. The seeds sown in the Reformation were watered by the chaos of revolution.

The immediate work of the Restoration was to dissolve the impact of the Commonwealth and this involved the re-establishment of the Anglican Church, as far as it was possible. Church courts were revived but they lost the vigour they had before. Estates that could be returned to the Church were. Plans for the augmentation of poor livings and reorganisation of the medieval parish structure were abandoned.

The more subtle effects of the upheaval could not be counteracted. The freedom to pursue new ways of religious observance, which many had seized during the Interregnum, would not disappear. The major groups of dissenters – Quakers, Baptists, Presbyterians and Congregationalists – remained in spite of a newly powerful Established Church and the prospect of persecution. Men and women attended the tiny but slowly growing number of chapels, appointed and paid for their chapel ministers and slowly moved outside the parish structure. The vast majority still attended their parish church and in 1662 chapel ministers were made subject to the approval of the parish's rector or vicar, but a sense of independence was now firmly in place.

It was cemented still further when, in 1688, a Dutch Calvinist ascended to the position of the supreme head of the Church of England and, twenty-six years later, a German Lutheran did the same thing. The Act of Toleration became a necessity. Nonconformist meeting houses were legalised. Only Catholics and Unitarians were still proscribed.

The Compton Census compiled in 1676 by the Anglican Church showed that nearly one in twenty adults was now nonconformist, which at that stage meant groups with roots in the Puritan wing of the Established Church. Another survey carried out between 1715–18 showed that the number of dissenting congregations was 1,934 and nonconformists comprised about 6 per cent of the population. It was not until Methodism exposed the chronic

Anglican weakness in new towns later in the century that dissention grew significantly in numbers.

However, even when numbers were comparatively small, the effect of nonconformism on the parish system was significant. Nonconformists naturally tended to gravitate to areas where Anglicanism was weaker. Presbyterians, for example, often exploited voids and weaknesses in the parish system by laying claim to territories and buildings that were moribund. The Quakers benefited from a strong organisational skill and enthusiasm and by 1700 they were more evenly distributed over the country than any other dissenting denomination.

In particular, and setting a precedent for later dissenters, nonconformity displayed its greatest strength in towns. By 1715 more than half of all Presbyterian, Independent and Baptist congregations were meeting in cities, boroughs or market towns, a vastly disproportionate figure given that only a fifth of the population was urban at this stage. Their rural impact was less noticeable, limited as it was by their being thinly spread, which made problems for fund-raising, and by the pressure to conform which was often imposed on them if there were a single Anglican landowner in the vicinity.

At first, many early meeting houses were domestic homes. Not until the Riot Act of 1715 was the wrecking of meeting houses made a felony and a significant number of chapels were built. Nevertheless, it was with the dissenters that the seeds sown by the Reformation and watered by the revolution first began to sprout and slowly, with great difficulty, break up the rigid structure of the parish system.

The Eighteenth Century

The number of nonconformist chapels built in the fifty years after the Act of Toleration was comparatively small. It was, instead, the lethargy and indolence of the Established Church that indirectly eroded the parish system by undermining its purpose and efficiency.

In 1709 Jonathan Swift noted that the recent growth of many towns had not been accompanied by any corresponding increase in the number of churches. He estimated (and probably exaggerated) that in places five in six people were prevented from attending a divine service.

Parliament responded in 1711 with what can only be described as comically slow and ineffective propriety. Motivated primarily by a fear that parishioners were falling into dissenting clutches, Parliament established a Commission for Building Fifty New Churches. This was to remain active for the next twenty-three years but in that time only managed to erect a total of nineteen new places of worship. Financial problems stopped the programme.

Anglican legalism and hopeless inflexibility left the country open for other denominations, but that was only part of the story. Even if popular ideas of the Established Church's corrupt lethargy during this period are sometimes overstated, there is little doubt that the age was one of misplaced priorities. Many vicars led a life of considerable comfort, as Parson Woodeford's famous diary illustrates. The clergy were better known for biology, classics and literature than their pastoral efforts.

Most notoriously, the Anglican Church was a den of pluralism, in which many clergymen received the income from several parishes while enjoying an easy life in trendy towns far away, and (under)paying a curate to do their work for them. In the diocese of Norwich a questionnaire of 1784 revealed that there were 128 incumbents resident in benefice with the other 285 served by a curate, of which 78 per cent had more than one parish. Revenue took precedence over souls.

It was in this atmosphere of idleness and carelessness that nonconformist chapels sprang up. Spiritually unfed and pastorally ignored, more and more parishioners were caught up in the Wesley movement and found themselves attending dissenting chapels.

Dissenters were not trapped by the rigidity of the parish system. Methodist preachers roamed over the landscape. Meeting houses were opened and discarded at will. Houses, halls and churches were borrowed and converted, or, failing that, open air meetings were held.

The initial uncertainty as to what Methodism actually was – was it a new way of Anglicanism or an entirely separate denomination? – resulted in an initial hesitation to erect new, purpose-built places of worship. It was not until the end of the eighteenth century that a category of specialised Methodist chapels began to emerge.

Even when these new buildings did begin to appear alongside already ancient Anglican churches, nonconformism retained a guerrilla element. Towards the end of the eighteenth century, a number of dissenting men and women, aware of the departure from the initial spirit of frugality and opportunism that had dominated early Methodism, initiated a second revival, partly fed by the millenarian fervour of the 1790s.

This 'Primitive Methodism', also known as 'Ranting', was virtually free from any authoritarian, paternalistic or establishment element and was, predictably, especially popular among the lower classes. Like the early Methodists, 'Primitive Methodists' met informally, their chapels starting out as cart-sheds, joiners' shops, forges, haylofts and converted houses. In time, they too established chapels, although without the rigour of the mainstream Methodists. Between them and the earlier dissenters, the established parish system was paralysed and slowly overwhelmed.

By the dawn of the nineteenth century, energetic non-conformism and lethargic Anglicanism had combined to transform the ecclesiastical landscape of England. Most parish churches had a small congregation of Methodists, Presbyterians, Baptists, Quakers, or some other group within shouting distance, with the only exceptions being particularly conservative, closed villages.

The Industrial Revolution, at least at first, exacerbated this situation enormously, primarily by instigating the biggest population shift in the country's history. Poverty, depression and opportunity drove and drew thousands out of the country into burgeoning towns and cities. The nonconformists' natural enthusiasm and flexibility allowed them to capitalise on these changes while the Anglicans were hamstrung by legal minutiae, conservatism, vested interests and spiritual torpor.

Towns that industrialised early tended to be woefully under-churched because the Established Church was reluctant or unable to split parishes, and nonconformists were yet to build their chapels. The contrast with the expanding post Norman Conquest towns, which were woefully over-churched because of the ecclesiastical eagerness and flexibility, could not be greater. In Liverpool, for example, where until the end of the seventeenth century there was only one parochial chapel, and that of medieval origin, population growth was so strong that by 1780 the population of 34,000 enjoyed a ratio of one Anglican church per 6,000 inhabitants. The next fifty years saw a concerted building programme by the Established Church but the ratio did not improve. The population far outpaced Anglican efforts and by 1830 the ratio had increased to one per 12,000.

The same story could be told of any number of industrial towns. Inflexibility and intransigence effectively disabled the Established Church and made the parish system at best inadequate and at worst an irrelevance. The eighteenth century saw a limited number of new parishes created in places where growth was exceptionally rapid but by the time Queen Victoria ascended to the throne, it appeared to be too little, too late. The parish system was dying.

Further Reading

Anthea Jones, *A Thousand Years of the English Parish: Medieval Patterns & Modern Interpretations* (Moreton-in-Marsh: Windrush, 2000)

Richard Morris, *Churches in the Landscape* (London: Phoenix, 1997)

Nicholas Pounds, *The History of the English Parish* (Cambridge: Cambridge University Press, 2000)

2

Crushed By Our Own Heritage

All Change in the Nineteenth Century

In 1801 the population of England and Wales was just over nine million; double what it had been a century earlier. In the previous 100 years, the number of Anglican parish churches had risen by 285. In the same period the number of nonconformist churches and meeting houses had nearly doubled to reach 3,701 at the start of the century.

The problem for the parish came not so much from the population increase, however, but in the imbalance across different areas. The parish structure was rooted in an agricultural society that had remained largely constant over the last millennium with 90 per cent of the population living in the country. While the age-old ratio of approximately one church to 300 or 400 parishioners had doubled in the last hundred years, now that 30 per cent of population lived in towns and 11 per cent lived in towns with populations of 100,000 plus, that ratio was considerably worse in many places.

To compound the problem, the notable medieval towns, such as Norwich, Exeter and York, which had reasonably dense parishes structures, were not the ones that were growing. Instead, it was towns like Liverpool, Manchester and Birmingham, ones that had barely been villages a century ago where the strain was really felt. In York, in 1801, there were twenty-three Established churches for 30,000 people, a ratio of one Anglican church to 1,250 residents. In Liverpool, however, in the same year, eight Anglican churches served 250,000 people. At that time, eight of largest sixty-five conurbations had a ratio of one Anglican church to 8,000 people. This was where the legacy of the poor agricultural value and large size of many medieval parishes in the north particularly affected the Established Church.

The situation was not much better in the country. A survey in 1812 revealed that nearly 60 per cent of rural incumbents were not resident in their parish. Spiritual sustenance was far more likely to be found in nonconformist churches, where the legacy of the itinerant ministries of Howell Harris, George Whitfield and John Wesley was to be found. The 'enthusiasm' of the nonconformists may have been derided by the sophisticated wits of the establishment, but it possessed an energy and commitment that – as Hogarth's famous engravings of congregations snoring as the preacher droned on showed – was absent in Anglican congregations.

Fear of nonconformism's success had long plagued the Established Church but reform of the parish structure was a long time coming. In the first twenty years of the nineteenth century, the population of England and Wales would increase by another three million (a figure approximately equal to the total population in 1200 when there were approximately 8,000 parish churches). Over those two decades the number of Anglican churches increased by about 150.

Until the Church Building Act of 1818 it did not matter whether church coverage was any good or not. A

parish could only be divided by statute and it was nor-
mally necessary to obtain an Act of Parliament for the
construction of a new church. The expense and tedium
of these formalities, coupled with the inertia or active
resistance of clergy who did not want their comfortable
benefices disrupted, and the genuine problem of there
being benefices which were too poor to support an
incumbent, effectively crippled any attempt at reform.

Many people, however, not least the high churchmen
and evangelicals, recognised that new measures were
desperately needed and by 1810 reform on a wide range
of fronts was the subject of public discussion in parliament, press and court. When the Napoleonic wars
ended in 1815 the discussion became even more
pressing. The Church Building Act of 1818 established a
commission 'for building and promoting the building of
additional churches in populous parishes', and made
one million pounds available for this. By 1820, eighty-
five new churches had been provided for and in 1821–2
further acts extended the financial powers of the commission, assisted it to acquire sites, dismember overlarge
parishes and combat vested interests.

The following thirty years saw 612 new parishes
defined and nearly 2,000 new churches built, with the
emphasis being on the areas of greatest need in
Yorkshire, Lancashire, the Midlands and the suburbs of
London. Although much of the reason for this sea
change must be put at the door of Anglican fear of nonconformism, it should also be seen as the Established
Church putting its house in order after years of inertia.
Parishes were now designed so that the Victorian industrial underclass, who were too ill-educated to benefit
from the intellectual content of much Christian teaching,
might be served. There was a call for intimate buildings
'to get the people close to us if they are to understand

us',[8] but also for larger ones, so that men and women of different classes in society would be brought to meet in the same church, to counter the divisiveness of social class. Whereas the seating plan of a country church could be a microcosm of the social structure of the whole parish, new Victorian churches were less hierarchical.

A similar story could be told of the attack on pluralism. The criticism of the Church at the time of the Great Reform Bill in 1831–2 finally saw the issue of pluralities tackled. It was an issue that went all the way up the Church hierarchy, with nineteen bishops holding sixty-one pieces of preferment between them. Clergymen were first and foremost learned, well connected, socially acceptable, influential, sophisticated gentlemen. In 1827 there were 4,413 clergymen resident in a total of 10,533 benefices.

Unsurprisingly, they were increasingly unpopular with protesting orators, who, in the maelstrom of the 1820s and 1830s, shouted that the bones of Tory parsons would soon be rotting with Tory peers and Tory squires. People talked of Cromwell and the Commonwealth and the downfall of the old church.

The first bill to limit pluralities was proposed in 1831 by Archbishop Howley but it was the same Ecclesiastical Commission which set about adding parishes and building churches that finally attacked the problem. In 1838 the Pluralities Act was passed, limiting the number of benefices of any one incumbent to two, which were to be within ten miles of one another. Neither was to have a population of over 3,000 and their joint value could not exceed £1,000.

The early nineteenth century may have seen the first substantial structural change to the Established Church but it was still a long way from a revolution. The pace was still being set by dissenters who increased the number of meeting places from 3,700 in 1801 to 8,700 in 1839. Moreover, stronger denominations no longer built small chapels tucked away for reasons of protection and cheapness but larger, more imposing buildings on main thoroughfares. By 1851 the total number of dissenting and Roman Catholic churches outnumbered those of the Anglicans.

The one area where the Anglican parish structure remained intact and valid was in the country. Britain was the most industrialised and most urbanised country in the world at the time but 65 per cent of the population still lived in rural areas and these, although well served by other churches, remained primarily Anglican.

This was to change too, however. The 1860s saw the beginning of the decline of the village church, primarily because it saw the decline of the village. As the young moved out to towns for higher wages and more opportunities, village institutions declined. Farmland lost value and with it university colleges, squires, parsons and ecclesiastical commissioners lost rents and tithes, and church attendance fell.

More pointedly, in this period of agricultural depression where there were increasing disputes between landlords and land-workers, the clergy were usually on the landowner's side. This, combined with labourers' growing social and political consciousness, made the clergyman rather unpopular.

The Church was recognised and criticised for teaching social subservience and obedience. Writing of her childhood in the Oxfordshire hamlet of Lark Rise in the 1880s, Flora Thompson says of the local pastor, 'his favourite subject was the supreme rightness of the social order as it then existed. God, in His infinite wisdom, had appointed a place for every man, woman and child on this earth and it was their bounden duty to remain contentedly in their niches.'[9] Another critic was more forthright: '... horrid mockery to teach men how to die, I say teach them how to live and make their lot happier here on earth. Living in this world is a certainty.'[10]

The result was an angry anti-clerical campaign of the 1870s and an increasing inclination to stop attending church altogether. Evidence suggests that for the first time the chapel did not gain what the church lost. From the mid-1880s we hear of secularist lecturers who often gave talks on Sundays specifically to steer people away from church. Some senior clergymen, such as J.C. Ryle, the first Bishop of Liverpool, openly declared that the Anglican Church was reaping a just harvest of pluralities and non-residences, of borrowed sermons and locked churches.

As the century neared its end, it became evident that men and women, even in rural areas, had a diminishing sense of the duty towards the parish church and public worship. There were new habits and pastimes for the laity to enjoy and a growing disinclination to walk long distances, perhaps due to the advent of railways and bicycles. As a result, the last decades of the century saw the building of mission chapels to serve newly populous parishes. Echoing the medieval chapels of ease, except insofar as these new edifices were encouraged rather than tolerated by the authorities, the ecclesiastical landscape changed once again, with smaller more informal buildings being used to supplement large, central ones.

Another element within the changing Christian landscape was the creation in 1865 of the office of lay reader. Originally for certain big towns, the role was soon adopted in country parishes. The growing number of parish chapels, effectively Anglican models of cheap, small, lay-reader led nonconformist chapels, began to make staffing a real problem.

At first, many Anglicans were suspicious of lay preachers taking services in church. Some thought it illegal, some irreverent and some too much like nonconformism. Accordingly, in the 1870s, laymen tended to help out in Sunday school or local chapels rather than in the main parish church and were not allowed to preach or take services in consecrated buildings. Change was slow, but by 1883 there were 684 lay readers across the country.

If the countryside showed signs of stagnation, the town was doing the opposite. Migration, high birth rates and a slowly declining infant mortality rate concentrated the population increase in the towns and whereas the 18 million population of England and Wales in 1851 was balanced two to one in favour of country to town, by 1901, the 33 million population was three to one, town to country.

Even as new churches were built in conurbations, the speed with which cities grew outward meant that many had too many churches in the centre and not enough around the periphery. The Church of England estimated that it needed about seventy new parishes and ninety-seven new clergymen to accommodate 300,000 new people every year in later decades of the century. Stunningly, as the century wore on, they actually achieved this. Between 1840 and 1876 Anglicans built nearly 2,000 new churches and rebuilt or restored over 7,000 old ones at a cost of over £25 million, mostly from the pockets of parishioners. Between 1851 and 1881, when the population of towns doubled, the number of Anglican (and Catholic) churches also doubled (and the number of Free Church chapels almost trebled).

Increasingly, Anglican churches paralleled the old grass-roots growth of nonconformist chapels. In 1877, Bishop Jackson of London said that the sub-division of parishes was proceeding with such rapidity that no man went to bed at night knowing whose parish he might wake up in. Ironically, however, just as the church building programme started to match the natural population increase, for the first time in a thousand years there came to be a real difference between the number of people and the number of churchgoers in the population. Church attendance in towns began to fall significantly in the later decades of the nineteenth century and the bigger the town the more rapid the decline in religious practice.

The reasons for this decline are complex and still a matter for considerable debate, but at least one of the major reasons was the parish structure itself. At first, when the great explosion of Anglican churches was beginning, there seemed good evidence to suggest that more churches meant more worshippers. There seemed an incontrovertible logic to this. The dearth of seating in Anglican churches, particularly in urban areas, was widely recognised and in so far as could be ascertained, attendance closely correlated with seating availability. Conclusion: build more churches.

The logic was not incontrovertible, however. More churches did appear, at first, to lead to more worshippers but the building of new parish churches did not occur in a vacuum. First, while the Anglicans frantically opened new places of worship, the Free Churches emulated and actually outpaced them. Secondly, the intellectual and social climate that underpinned attendance at the parish church was changing. The embryonic socialist movement offered, so it seemed to many working class men, far more hope and support for their future. Hard-pressed workers, long since frustrated by the traditional 'you'll get your rewards in the next life' line, increasingly had some socially acceptable alternative to which to turn. Thirdly, shrinking congregations gave off an odour of failure. A half-empty church subtly spoke of the 50 per cent of people who knew better or had things that they would rather be doing. A half-empty church also demanded twice the effort from the congregation just to keep going and made attracting new members doubly difficult. Mission became impossible when maintenance became so demanding. And when a half-empty church is interpreted as a sign of secularisation, secularisation can become a self-fulfilling prophecy. Half-emptiness sets the precedent for emptiness.

This left the Anglicans with a real problem, but, crucially for later generations, its severity could be deferred. Being the Established Church, close to the seat of power and with enormous revenues on which it could draw, the Church of England could tolerate levels of expansion that led to ever more sparse congregations. The late nineteenth century gave rise to the phenomenon of subsidised inefficiency which remains central to the Church of England's problems today. Dwindling congregations were by no means ideal, but they did not affect the budget too badly.

Free Churches, on the other hand, could not draw the same comfort. They had outpaced the Anglican expansion – the Methodists had consciously tried to emulate the Established Church's national coverage – and hence faced the same problem, only more seriously. For them the implications came rather sooner. They simply could not subsidise small congregations with existing funds. As the number of congregations increased, their size decreased. This made large chapels less viable and led to increased diffusion and a growth of smaller chapels. But smaller chapels had smaller congregations that were even more financially precarious. Free Churches simply could not pay for themselves. The massive reduction in nonconformist chapels in the early decades of the twentieth century were what the Anglican Church would have faced had it not been cushioned by massive financial investments.

The rising level of lay responsibility in Anglican parishes compounded Free Church economic problems. The opportunity to take a more active part in an Anglican congregation removed one of the main attractions of nonconformism and contributed to the slow decline of the Free Churches in the twentieth century.

These two problems resulted in something of a vicious spiral. Dire financial straits, small and little-used chapels, and the growing attraction of other denominations led the Methodists to stretch their stipendiary ministers over larger and larger circuits, rely upon an ageing lay leadership and, at the last resort, close many chapels across the country. The decay, destruction and conversion of thousands of small chapels across England and Wales in the early twentieth century offers a sobering message for those concerned with the future of the Anglican parish church.

The Catholic Church alone avoided this process of decay. The late nineteenth and early twentieth centuries were a time of revival for the Catholic Church in Britain, mainly as a result of immigration. In the period from 1861 to 1901, the number of Catholic churches rose from 798 to 1,536, a rate commensurate with the increase in Anglican churches, but with several important differences.

First, the massive influx of Catholic immigrants, especially from Ireland, meant that the growth in churches did not outpace the growth in potential worshippers, as it did elsewhere. Secondly, the immigrant nature of the Catholic worshippers naturally lent itself to more committed congregations. Catholics would travel a long way to church, simply because it meant so much more to them than many of their Anglican peers. Finally, theological differences meant that the structure of the Catholic network was fundamentally very different to that of other denominations, a fact which will be discussed in a later chapter.

As the twentieth century subsequently showed, these differentiating factors were not going to remain forever. A far-sighted writer in *The Catholic Times* wrote in 1891 that 'whilst the poor Catholics who came over from Ireland, with their strong faith, in a strange land, and surrounded by poverty, made heroic efforts to hear Mass, [today] many of their children who are in better circumstances and better educated do not attend Mass in the same way'. It was to be nearly a century – and a good fifty years after other denominations – before the Catholic Church in Britain would realise these prophetic words of decline.

The nineteenth century witnessed the fastest and most important change in the history of the English ecclesiastical landscape. A vast number of churches were built by all denominations. Parish churches appeared in Victoria's reign with a breadth and frequency unequalled in 1,000 years. But the changing nature of church attendance meant that many new churches were left half full. Parish loyalties were still very strong in rural areas but rural areas themselves were declining, supporting fewer people and less work. The town was the landscape of the future and despite, or perhaps because of the churches' best efforts in urban areas, the parish never attained much meaning for or the loyalty of town dwellers in the same way as it had in the country.

The Upheaval of Wars

The story of the decline of the parish in England in the twentieth century is overshadowed by the decline of

Christianity and the emergence of the phenomenon that has been called 'believing without belonging'.

The secularisation of Britain has been variously dated to anywhere between the mid-eighteenth century and 1963. With religiosity being so difficult to measure accurately, debates over the precise nature and extent of secularisation are unlikely to reach a conclusion. In the decade following Queen Victoria's death, there were around twenty-three million baptised Anglicans in the United Kingdom, of whom slightly over three million, or 9 per cent, attended church. The other religious communities comprised a further three-and-a-half million worshippers. On an average Sunday, you would expect to find one in five of the population in church.

The Established Church may have still been at the heart of power but anyone who ventured any distance from Westminster got a rather different picture. Even in rural areas, long the stronghold of Anglicanism, the condition of spiritual life was questionable, fairly described by the historian Roger Lloyd as the 'passive acquiescence in traditional religion [rather] than a triumphant living faith'.[11] This was evident in a unique survey of the religious knowledge, beliefs and attitudes of trench soldiers in the First World War. Conducted by army chaplains and published at the end of the war, this report revealed a distinctly sub-Christian picture.

The chaplains estimated that whereas four-fifths of the men had been to Sunday school, a similar proportion did not subsequently go to church. Just over one in ten English soldiers (and twice as many Scots) were in, what they called, a 'vital relationship' with a church. Catholic soldiers attended church more regularly than non-Catholics.

Non-attendance did not equal non-belief, however. The survey found that most soldiers believed in God and also prayed. This undoubtedly had much to do with the unthinkable situations in which the troops found themselves, as the authors recognised. Scientific materialism did not offer much solace when going over the top:

> The men of the British armies, however dim their faith may be, do in the hour of danger, at least, believe in God, 'the great and terrible God'. Most men we are told pray before they go over the parapet, or advance in the face of machine guns, and they thank God when they have come through the battle ... men believe that there is an Unseen Power, inaccessible to the senses, which is yet mightier than high explosives, which knows all and which hears prayer.[12]

Such beliefs, forged in the fires of the front, were highly instinctive. As with their general idea of an afterlife, soldiers naturally drew on the Christian worldview and vocabulary with which most of them had grown up. But there was more than a little patriotism mixed in with the theology: 'The idea of salvation by death in battle for one's country has been widely prevalent, and is one of those points in which the religion of the trenches has rather a Moslem than a Christian colour.'[13]

In spite of these quasi-Christian beliefs, the report recorded a widespread disaffection with the Church. While the authors found that there was 'not much . . . reasoned unbelief', there was the sense that 'the Churches are afraid to face the whole truth . . . services are unreal [and] preachers have no real contact with human life'.[14] More typically, there was the accusation of failure to do the very thing they were supposed to. 'Whether the charge be of the lack of fellowship within the Churches, or of their want of human sympathy with the disinherited classes, or of the divisions between different communions, it is an accusation of lack of love.'[15]

Overall the summary is uncannily familiar to twenty-first-century ears:

> [The soldiers had the impression] that there is little or no life in the Church at all, that it is an antiquated and decaying institution, standing by dogmas expressed in archaic language, and utterly out of touch with modern thought and living experience ... they believe that the Churches are more and more governed by the middle-aged and the elderly; they think ministry professionalised and out of touch with the life of men, deferring unduly to wealth ... They say they do not see any real differences in the strength and purity of life between the people who go to church and the people who do not.[16]

In the face of such sobering findings the Church was making changes – slowly. The problem had many roots, but one of the deepest was a pastoral system that creaked with history and subtly inhibited the gospel. At best, it favoured pastoral work over essential evangelism. At worst, it dug its heels in against all change.

The need had been recognised by some perceptive individuals for some time. There was little hope when the Church was faced with buildings that were on average less than half full and a parish system which, in the words of Charles Booth, 'render[ed] the position of the clergy and their co-workers, very impracticable'.

The evident missionary need was also hampered by a deficit of clergy. This was calculated at over 5,000 in 1908 and increased by a further 2,000 in the succeeding two decades, prompting the anonymous editor of *Crockford's Clerical Directory* to write, in 1927: 'it is not too much to say that if the history of the last ten years is continued for another ten the effective maintenance of the parochial system will have become impossible in all but a few favoured localities'.[17] What was needed, so argued one writer, was a new system of pluralities. Unfortunately, and somewhat ironically, the reforming 1838 Act effectively prohibited this and necessitated a special Act of Parliament to get exemptions.

Inasmuch as there was change, it was not unusual in rural areas for a parish to be merged with its neighbour on the retirement or death of an incumbent. The problem was that this could only ever be an ad hoc measure, devoid of any systematic strategy. The idea of deliberately working groups of country parishes together with a single staff centre was decades away.

It should be stressed that these problems did not completely prevent churches from carrying out their pastoral ministry. The parish system may have been ordered (or perhaps disordered) so as to nurse individualism and hamper cooperation, but it failed to dampen much of the activity that marked the opening decades of the century. In the long term, pastors may have been living on the Titanic, but they were doing a lot of good there: the Mother's Union, the Church of England Men's Society, the Girls' Friendly Society, the Band of Hope, the King's Messengers, house-to-house visiting, social clubs, and the ceaseless relief of the poor, hungry and homeless demanded the energy and received the exhaustion of many clergymen. In the pre-war period, and particularly before the state stepped in with old age pensions and a system of benefit for the sick, much of the social burden fell and was ably borne by parish churches.

Congregation sizes actually increased in the early decades of the century but there was still a sense of running to stand to still. As the state provided more and more for society, parishes were either evicted from their role or compelled to become better organised and more 'business-like' in their affairs, a demand which was foreign to the haphazard organisation of their ministry. The removal of ad hoc relief work from the churches emptied them of some of their purpose, just as Victorian parish reforms had done at the end of the nineteenth century. Because so much more energy had been expended on pastoral work than on mission, when the social role dwindled, parish congregations did too. The Church had fulfilled its traditional, pastoral role at the expense of attending to its foundations.

Nevertheless, some measures were taken. Largely through the efforts of the future archbishop William Temple, the Life and Liberty movement secured the Enabling Act of 1919 that allowed the Anglican Church much needed freedom to manage its own affairs. Ruridecanal conferences, brought into existence by the Enabling Act, helped break down the isolation between one village and an-other. The Church started to address the issue of vast, unwieldy, expensive country rectories. The decline in clergy and finances which made it increasingly difficult to operate one parson one parish, led to more and more benefices being united.

Non-parochial ministries also developed rapidly. The Industrial Christian Fellowship was set up in 1919, in the important recognition that 'if the parish is no longer always the natural unit for expressing community, then the office, factory, or industrial complex where people work will provide the sense of community which they will not find elsewhere'.[18]

Modern cell and house groups also have their roots in this inter-war period, with a number of priests recognising the power of the small group and encouraged parishioners (or factory workers) to meet together, often in each other's houses, and pray. For some this was a conscious imitation of the early church; for others it was an imitation of the cellular expansion of the communists; and for others it was a deliberate revolt against the organised church. Whatever the reason, it was soon discovered that the house church made the parish church more, rather than less, used.

After the War

The Second World War disturbed parish life just as it disrupted everything else. Few parish churches ended the war with more than a fraction of the regular worshippers they had when it began. In the longer term, the war acted as a catalyst for the social changes that had been gathering pace during the inter-war years.

Looking back over the immediate post-war period from the vantage point of the early 1960s, the sociologist Leslie Paul recorded the multitude of social changes that were straining the parish system almost to breaking point. The population was rapidly increasing and the geographic and demographic profile of the country was changing equally fast. Slum clearances, farm mechanisation, youth exoduses, and factory, pit and rail closures were shutting down areas. Immigration, retirement and tourism were changing the profile of others. Road building schemes, business relocation and new housing were opening up new areas altogether. The face of the country was changing.

The growth of new towns was particularly important, because, in the ever more mobile, rootless and atomised post-war years, these new communities never really became communities. New residents had very little sense of belonging and often spent more time away from home, working, shopping and relaxing, than they did at home. The historical role of the church as community centre was thwarted even before a new incumbency had been carved out of the local parishes. As Leslie Paul said, 'the Church cannot be an integral part of what does not exist'.[19]

At the same time, the intellectual climate in which Christianity operated was changing radically. In 1947, a Mass Observation report recorded that

> both in regard to formal observances and general attitude, the younger generation show a much more critical outlook, and much less interest [in religion]. Two young people (under forty) express doubt about the existence of God for every older person who does so. It is mostly the younger generation who dismiss religion with apparent disinterest.[20]

Such views became more common in the 1960s when a pot-pourri of various ill-thought out, hopelessly idealistic, naïve, drug-fuelled, self-centred utopias competed for the attention and money of the newly affluent and influential youth.

The parish church struggled to cope with these upheavals. The Church was low on vicars and those it did have were poorly used, with half of the Anglican benefices covering 10 per cent of the population in the early 1960s. The result was a catastrophic imbalance of work, so that one urban incumbent could write in the early 1960s, 'the parish will literally kill me one day and I am quite prepared for this', while another rural one could say, 'the amount contributed for all Church purposes last year was £23. I have had five confirmation candidates in seventeen years. There is no PCC, no organist, no choir and no verger. There is no heating in winter.' Both were extreme but neither was unique.

At the same time, the Sunday school movement went into meltdown, with the estimated 30 per cent of three-to-fourteen-year-olds who attended a Sunday school in 1910 becoming 15 per cent by 1958 and 2.5 per cent by 1989. Anglican Church attendance did not drop quite so savagely but still fell steadily, from an average 3.5 per cent of the population attending an Established Church every Sunday in 1968, to 1.9 per cent in 1999.

In the midst of these dramatic changes, the Church of England slowly began to loosen its parish structure. A series of measures – New Parishes Measure (1943), Reorganisation of Areas Measure (1944), Pastoral Reorganisation Measure (1949), Benefice (Suspension of Presentation) Measure (1949, 1952), New Housing Areas (Church Buildings) Measure (1954) – passed by the Church Assembly made reorganisation schemes, the creation of new parishes, the union of benefices and the holding of benefices in plurality possible. Flexibility was beginning to replace rigidity.

Even when amalgamated, however, parishes still maintained separate parochial institutions and although vicars were not legally obliged to provide two sets of Sunday services, many tried to. On top of this, there was often perceived to be an unfair advantage for those parishes in which the vicar was resident, a perception that bred understandable resentment. Overall, amalgamation was a necessary rather than a popular move, reflected in the comment in the 1955 *Crockford's*: 'We recognise the regrettable necessity which has caused many of these schemes, but they seem to us to have become a holy passion with some bishops and archdeacons, who roam the countryside seeking what parishes they may devour.'[21]

Rural areas, which most needed and most endured these measures, were also the most reluctant to adopt them. As Paul Welsby wrote in his history of the post-war Church of England, 'their innate conservatism [led] country church people to cling to the conception that every village should have its own resident parson, little realising that this was an idea of recent origin'.[22]

Some relief to this tension was found in the implementation of the Christian Stewardship movement which was adopted by hundreds of parishes from 1954 onwards. This had started in New Zealand and the USA ten years earlier and rested on the principle that the whole congregation should share responsibility and costs. All parishioners must know what was needed, how much it cost and how this money was to be provided, with clergy and laity acting and budgeting together.

This was essentially an extension of the laity's already growing role in the everyday life of the church and helped produce a new understanding of laity in church. Accredited lay ministries proliferated and the laity had begun to share in decision making at parochial and higher levels. Hans Rudi Weber wrote in *The Layman's Church* in 1963: 'The laity are not the helpers of the clergy so that the clergy can do their job but the clergy are the helpers of the whole people of God, so that the laity can be the Church.' Vicar-less churches were less of a burden if congregations were effectively running the establishment in the first place.

Increased lay participation was only part of the solution, however. Official measures were still needed. When the Pastoral Measure was passed in 1968, after having been before the Church Assembly for four years, it amended the law of pluralities and the union of parishes and benefices, enabling parishes to be created without a parish church, and provided for setting up of team and group ministries and for alteration of ecclesiastical boundaries. It also dealt with preservation and disposal of redundant churches.

The measure created tensions between dioceses which could see the whole picture and parishes who had and wished to preserve their own local concerns and identity, but overall the measure helped improve the Church's pastoral ability, and although change was slow, the 1970s and 1980s saw the growth of new parish schemes and the slow accumulation of redundant churches across the country.

The Bell Tolling

Unfortunately, the Pastoral Measure did little to stop the ebbing tide of worshippers. The late 1970s witnessed a small and brief recovery in church attendance figures, more of a slowing in the rate of decline than a revival, but the 1980s and 1990s – despite the latter being the much-trumpeted Decade of Evangelism – was a time of seemingly relentless decline.

Culturally, too, these were the decades when Christianity's influence declined massively. The nuclear family (albeit a relatively recent phenomenon, appropriated by the Victorians and canonised as the necessary bedrock of any stable, Christian society) began to fissure. All authority figures became suspect. 'Giving a moral lead' was now deeply unfashionable or, worse, deemed fascistic. An increasingly cosmopolitan population started to engage with other religious traditions. Even though there was nothing substantial or universally recognised to replace it, the pseudo-Christian mindset that had underpinned the largely non-churchgoing population for much of the twentieth century was decaying fast.

In the long run, this cultural decline may have been the best thing that could have happened to the Church. A nation that lost any real understanding of the gospel but maintained a distinctly sub-Christian concept of the faith as a peculiarly English mix of decency, morality, authority, eternity, nationality and tradition, had effectively, indeed almost literally, been inoculated against Jesus Christ. The population received, at weddings, funeral, baptisms, Christmases, and the occasional Easter, just enough of this slightly corrupted version of religion, to become immune to the real thing. As one young respondent, interviewed as part of research conducted by The London Institute for Contemporary Christianity into religious belief in Britain today, said of the future of Christianity in Britain:

> Perhaps with us not being so religious as a generation we won't … pass on these negative things attached to religion to our children … We see religion as quite stuffy, old fashioned … so we don't go … our children, or our children's children won't have been brought up on those beliefs so they might adopt it.[23]

Reassuring as such a long-term view may be, it contains an enormous 'if' and does little to help ease the strain on pastors and parishes. For both congregations and ministers the story was a grim one. Overall church attendance fell from around 11 per cent of the population in 1980 to under 8 per cent at the millennium.

In the same period, weekly adult Anglican Church attendance fell from a million to under 800,000. Children's attendance fell between one-quarter and one-third in the 1990s. New counting methods adopted in the new century to reflect people's more fluid, less frequent church attendance suggested attendance levels were actually slightly higher and pushed the overall level up to around 1.3 million. Irrespective of this, however, the news was not encouraging. 'More people on Titanic than first thought', as one wag put it.

As the nation left Christian culture behind it, the formal passages of Christian life declined. The 25 million-strong Anglican 'community' in Britain (essentially the number of people baptised) included a high proportion of people who had been baptised by their parents because it was the done thing. As the millennium approached this 'community' began to decline. The number of infant baptisms fell 13 per cent in the 1980s and a further 24 per cent in the 1990s. Changes in marriage laws had the same effect on church weddings.

The number of full-time clergy also fell, from just over 11,000 in 1990 to around 9,000 in 2000, and this was in spite of the decision to ordain women, who currently make up a sixth of all Church of England ministers. Inevitably, the fewer clergy endured heavier workloads and greater levels of stress and anxiety. The situation showed few signs of improving, with ordinations falling from 361 in 1990 to 313 in 2000. To top this, the 1990s saw the Church lose nearly a billion pounds in investments, making the fall in the number of stipends something of an ironic blessing.

One figure did resist decline in this period though – the number of churches. Over these decades the number of Anglican churches hardly fell at all. A tiny number of buildings actually closed but the majority managed to remain open, many in some truncated, poverty-stricken, minister-less form. The pattern of a stagnant network supporting an ever-lighter burden of parishioners that marked the twentieth century carried through right to the end. It became a classic example of disaster management but one that, as Bob Jackson has observed, simply cannot be maintained into the twenty-first century: 'An ever-dwindling number of Anglicans cannot keep the same number of buildings going indefinitely. Eventually, fewer and fewer Anglicans will have no time left for anything else – we will be crushed by our own heritage.'[24]

Overall, the news may be discouraging but it is important to balance it with other trends. Many of the more encouraging phenomena were natural concomitants of a nation throwing off the remnants of its already dead beliefs, or, to use a more biblical metaphor, of an old vine being ruthlessly pruned. As the number of infant baptisms fell, the number of other age groups being baptised increased, with the number of adult baptisms rising to over 10,000 in 1999. There has been an increase in non-stipendiary ministers and lay readers. Necessity has increased the pace of pastoral reorganisation, giving impetus to the development of diocesan-sponsored local ministry teams in order to transfer ministry and workload to people who are unpaid but trained. More money is also being given, and that by fewer worshippers. More churchgoers are going to midweek meetings and with the success of Alpha, Emmaus and other process evangelism courses, the Church (in all its denominations) is a more evangelism-shaped organisation.

However, as the opening years of the twenty-first century progress, the future does not look bright. The task before the Church is vast, complex and without any obvious solution. Indeed, being at least as much cultural as it is organisational, there are some things the Church will have no control over. But, where it can, it needs to put its own house in order, at least before that house falls down around its ears.

The History of the Parish – A Brief Conclusion

At the turn of the twenty-first century, the Church matters less in people's lives than it has done at any time over the last 1,000 years. Most people neither know nor care which parish they are resident in.

For 500 years, the parish had been a natural community in rural areas. It may have originally been a secular unit, it may have evolved in the most ad hoc manner, there may have been a multitude of stresses and strains that twisted and tweaked the structure here and there, but the power of authority kept it in place. Overall, it worked.

Even when this supreme authority had been replaced (albeit with another supreme authority), no one at any point attempted to dismantle it, outside some ambitious and ineffectual thoughts during the turmoil of the seventeenth century. Once the seeds of reformation had been sown, however, it was only a matter of time before the parish became redundant. A small number of people opted out of the whole system. Those who remained within it were less intrinsically involved with the spiritual life of the parish, after the altars had been stripped, rural customs been banned and the ecclesiastical authority which kept the parish system from splintering in the Middle Ages fatally undermined. The parish may still have been an administrative centre of the countryside but that was just about all that held it together.

Peace and tolerance brought apathy and abuse in the eighteenth century. The dissent this provoked benefited, at first, from being flexible and having no rigid structure to conform to. Once it became clear that the Anglican Church was unwilling to reform and adapt to the new environment, nonconformism sunk tangible roots in the landscape.

The process of industrialisation and urbanisation highlighted the inadequacies of the official parish structure and the successes of nonconformist fluidity. Although fear, external pressure and, ultimately, reforming zeal did finally motivate a great deal of parochial reform under Queen Victoria, it was too much too late. The rural areas that were still suited to the old parish became less populous and more antagonistic to the structure and teaching of the Established Church, and growing secularisation undermined the heroic building activities of the late Victorians.

At the same time, with the creation of urban and rural district parish councils in 1888 and 1894, the Victorians removed the civil duties and administrative functions from the parish that the Tudors had placed there 300 years previous. This withdrawal of secular business left the vestry without life. By the end of the nineteenth century, rural environments were diminishing in people, size and function, and the growing urban ones were ill suited or ill served. The ancient English parish was on its last legs.

What is really surprising is that it has taken such a long time to die. The prospects did not look great in 1900 and yet a century later we are still resolutely parochial. This is partly due to the deep roots of the parish structure – many non-churchgoers defend their little local parish church with considerable ferocity – and also to the significant efforts expended by many Christians throughout the later nineteenth and twentieth centuries to refill the churches.

Ultimately, the problems were more profound, as Robin Gill points out:

> Despite the considerable rhetoric typically made by denominations about mission and evangelism, their deep-seated structural problems would have ensured that they continued to decline throughout the twentieth century. Both the heavily subsidized Church of England and the over-extended Free Churches, would – unless

their structures were radically transformed – have continued to decline in an entirely predictable way.[25]

The deep roots that have kept the parish structure alive for so much longer than might have been predicted a century ago are also the reason why, ultimately, it cannot survive. The affection and care with which we deal with parishes allows churches to plan for their own decline without realising it. History counsels against making predictions but there does not seem much prospect of the English parish existing in the same way as it does now a hundred years hence. A new model is needed.

Further Reading

Owen Chadwick, *The Victorian Church* (2 Vols; London: A. & C. Black, 1970–2)

Monica Furlong, *C of E: The State It's In* (London: Hodder & Stoughton, 2000)

Robin Gill, *The Empty Church Revisited* (London: SPCK, 2003)

Roger Lloyd, *The Church of England 1900–1965* (London: SCM, 1966)

Paul Welsby, *A History of the Church of England 1945–1980* (Oxford: Oxford University Press, 1984)

3

The Minster Church

The Age of 'Conversion'

If you had happened to visit Thanet in the summer of 1997 you might have stumbled upon the somewhat peculiar sight of a large group of middle-aged, purple-robed men paddling in the water. These men, among them George Carey, then Archbishop of Canterbury, were walking shoreward, in memory of St Augustine and his Italian clerics who, 1,400 years previously, had landed in the kingdom of Aethelbert of Kent and begun the conversion of Britain.

In fact, Britain had adopted Christianity along with the rest of the Roman Empire over quarter of a millennium earlier when Emperor Constantine had seen a cross in the sky just before the battle of Milvian Bridge. In a typically astute move, he became a Christian, taking millions of pagans and the Empire with him.

With the crumbling of the Roman Empire in the fifth century, Christianity declined in Britain. The legions left in 410, the economy collapsed, towns decayed, and over the next century pagan Germanic invaders asserted their

supremacy. British Christians were forced westwards
and northwards.

When, nearly two centuries later, Pope Gregory the
Great instigated Augustine's mission, he had mapped
out the ecclesiastical pattern of the to-be-converted
nation on what appears to have been a Roman plan. His
original scheme had been to establish two provinces in
the nation, ruled by archbishops based in London and
York, with each overseeing twelve sees. It is an indica-
tion of how much things had changed that this never
even looked likely to happen.

Augustine's mission was initially successful, with
Kent and Essex becoming Christian within a decade and
inroads being made into East Anglia. The sees of
Canterbury, Rochester and London were successfully set
up but when Aethelbert, the supportive King of Kent
died in 616, Augustine's mission (outside Kent) effectively died with him.

It was in the following half century that most of the
kings of England were converted, with much of the successful missionary work conducted by 'Celtic' Christians. In 686, the Isle of Wight became the last English
kingdom to turn to Christ.

The conversion had not gone to plan and nor did the
administrative strategy. Canterbury became the
supreme archbishopric and the country was not divided
in anything like as orderly a way as Gregory had antici-
pated. When the sixty-seven-year-old Theodore of
Tarsus arrived to take up the archbishopric of
Canterbury in 669, there were only seven dioceses in
existence, only four of these being occupied, and none
by an uncontroversial bishop. The pastoral affairs for the
newly converted nation were, as the historian James
Campbell has put it, in a state of 'diversity amounting to
chaos'.[26]

This state of chaotic diversity was addressed only slowly. The first English church council, held at Hertford in 672 declared that 'more bishops be created as the number of the faithful increases'. By the time Theodore died in 690 there were thirteen or fourteen sees, and forty years later when Bede was putting the finishing touches to his *Ecclesiastical History*, he listed twelve bishoprics in the southern kingdoms and four north of the Humber. Five years on, in 735, York eventually became the second metropolitan see.

Though sees gradually multiplied, their pastoral effectiveness was still questionable. Christianity was originally a primarily urban religion and bishoprics had been founded around the Mediterranean shore where cities were densely packed. In parts of North Africa a bishop would have overseen a small town of a few thousand souls.

Gregory's own experience of episcopal organisation had been in central and southern Italy, where bishoprics were based on Roman cities. His own *Book of Pastoral Rule* required that bishops closely supervise the spiritual health of their flock and remain humble amidst the pomp. Both these were objectives best served by the small diocese with which he was familiar, which allowed easier visitation and provided a smaller revenue.

The situation in Britain was rather different. Anglo-Saxon cities were non-existent and the remains of Roman ones were thinly distributed and in a state of severe disrepair. More importantly, Anglo-Saxon society was dominated by the members and ethos of a warrior aristocracy. These two facts had enormous impact on both the structure and style of episcopal government in England.

Sees tended to be based on kingdoms or sub-kingdoms. People had their own bishop. Bishops, more to the point, had their own people, and needed them. The early Anglo-Saxon bishop was a man born and bred in a culture of riches and retinues. A large see befitted the dignity of a nobleman bishop and carving it up to make more pastorally effective units was less important than maintaining its revenues for the bishop's honour. Multiplying sees was resisted not just by the geography of the land but also by its ecclesiastical culture.

This resulted in problems. A few years after he had finished his *Ecclesiastical History*, Bede wrote a letter to his former pupil, Egbert, soon to be Archbishop of York. In it he said what he had understated in his *Ecclesiastical History*. Vast and too few dioceses meant that a bishop, the indisputable head of the pastoral tree, was not able to discharge his duties properly. The people were not being spiritually fed:

> For we have heard ... that many villages and hamlets of our people are situated in inaccessible mountains and dense woodlands, where there is never seen for many years at a time a bishop to exhibit any ministry ... not one man of which, however, is immune from rendering dues to the bishop.[27]

It was because of this neglect that pastoral care in Anglo-Saxon England developed along the lines it did and owes at least as much to Celtic Christianity as it does to Augustine's mission.

The Minster Church

With the conversion of England came the foundation of monasteries. In the mid-seventh century there were no more than a handful of monasteries, but by the time of the first Viking raids, 150 years later, there were at least 200.

The word 'monastery' as we use it today carries with it a wide range of images and associations. In our mind's eye we tend to see the great buildings of later centuries, such as Fountains or Riveaux Abbey. We think of the strict, authoritarian regularity, as depicted in *The Name of the Rose* or the Brother Cadfael mysteries. Above all, we think of seclusion: men and women who have renounced the world and all it has to offer in favour of peace, isolation and contemplation. Yet, at least before the monastic reforms on the eve of the Norman Conquest, these definitions are ill suited to the Anglo-Saxon world, which saw institutions with a far more varied and pastorally minded concept of monasticism.

These were Anglo-Saxon 'minsters'. The word is simply a rendering of the Latin *monasterium* into Old English. Although soon passing out of common usage, the word is still seen in the names of a number of towns, villages and churches across the country. From Axminster in Devon up to Minsterley in Shropshire and across to Minster-in-Thanet and Minster-in-Sheppey in Kent, there are today a number of places that retain some sign of their Anglo-Saxon ecclesiastical past. York, Wimborne and Beverley minsters, to name but three, all retain their Anglo-Saxon heritage in their names.

Monasticism began in the late third century when a young man named Anthony decided to give away his possessions and live an isolated, ascetic existence in the Egyptian desert, and it flourished as a layman's quest for spiritual purity after the church became established under Constantine. Among the Celtic Christians based north and west of the Anglo-Saxon kingdoms, the monastery or minster was the primary unit of organisation and served as the Christian centre for a whole district. Being far less familiar with the Roman concept of the diocese, bishops in Celtic society were comparatively unimportant, and acted more as functionaries for ordaining and consecrating than as lynchpins of the entire pastoral system.

Accordingly, in Celtic society abbots had considerable authority within an area, and there was an active and reciprocal relationship between the 'mother churches' and their flocks. A church owed its people the duty of celebrating Mass, performing baptism, preaching the word and saying prayers for the dead. Failure to provide these would allow the people to withhold their tithes and first fruits. Certain early Irish laws went to the length of defining and legislating for this mutual relationship.

It was from these mother churches that missionaries would travel and bring the gospel to distant villages and hamlets. One of the most famous of the Celtic missionaries of the early period was St Cuthbert. He combined a life of ascetic isolation in Lindisfarne with a ministry that led him to travel to the most distant and neglected communities, teaching and preaching.

Although Anglo-Saxon England was Christianised primarily through this approach, rather than through Augustine, it would be a mistake to see the early English church as simply aping a Celtic Christianity and certainly not the saccharine, quasi-mystical, nature worshipping Celtic Christianity which is often portrayed today.

England was at a confluence and was shaped by Gallic and Roman Christianity just as much as it was by the Celtic variety. Monasteries of the more official, formal type were not unknown even in the early years, and the most famous Anglo-Saxon historian, Bede himself, was based in a large, conventional community in Monkwearmouth-Jarrow on the Tyne and Wear. Bede's home was a far larger, stricter and wealthier 'minster' than many others that were founded in the seventh and eighth centuries, some of which seem to have been staffed by no more than a handful of clergy.

And it is here that the first important characteristic of minsters emerges – their diversity. Although they did become something close to a coherent pastoral framework in later centuries, their origins in the seventh and eighth centuries were as ad-hoc as those the parish system would be 300 years later. Some were founded by royal edict, some by episcopal command and some were proprietary, belonging to aristocrats in much the same way as parish churches later would. Many were established for devotional rather than pastoral reasons, with wealthy founders wanting an impressive private chapel through which they might fulfil what they saw as their Christian duties.

Others had more official sanction, being established by royal grants of land, adjacent to centres of royal power, headed by royal abbots or abbesses, and with areas of responsibility defined by existing political or economic territories. They were, in essence, the ecclesiastical twin of the local secular power base.

Some, like Monkwearmouth-Jarrow, had more obvious ecclesiastical origins, representing an establishment founded partly according to Benedictine principles and staffed by 'traditional' monks and abbots, dedicated to a life of study and prayer. But even among this group there was considerable variety, with male, female and double-houses, of differing sizes and wealth.

Inevitably, given the variety and freedom of origins, a number of minsters were of questionable status. Bede ended his *Ecclesiastical History* with a somewhat elliptical reference to them

> In these favourable times of peace and prosperity, many of the Northumbrian race, both noble and simple, have

laid aside their weapons and taken the tonsure, preferring that they and their children should take monastic
vows rather than train themselves in the art of war. What
the result will be, a later generation will discover.[28]

However, in the same letter to Egbert in which he
opened up about the lamentable pastoral record of certain bishops, Bede wrote at great length and candour
about the sham minsters that were appearing across the
country:

There are innumerable places allowed the name of
monasteries by a foolish manner of speaking, but having
nothing of a monastic way of life; some of which I would
wish to be transformed by synodal authority from wan-
ton living to chastity, from vanity to truth, from
overindulgence of the belly and from gluttony to conti-
nence and piety of heart ... [they are populated by]
whomsoever they may find wandering anywhere,
expelled from true monasteries for the fault of disobedi-
ence, or whom they can allure out of monasteries, or,
indeed, those of their own followers whom they can persuade to promise them the obedience of a monk and
receive the tonsure ... with the unseemly companies of
these persons they fill the monasteries which they have
built, and ... the very same men are now occupied with
wives and the procreation of children, now rising from
their beds to perform with assiduous attention what
should be done within the precinct of the monasteries ...
with like shamelessness they procure for their wives
places for constructing monasteries.[29]

This seems a pretty damning indictment, although one
has to be aware that Bede was writing from the stand-
point of lifelong commitment to one of the greatest and

strictest monasteries in the country. His other writings reveal his unwavering commitment to the most exacting standard among his fellow churchmen and the laity. His contempt for many minsters may simply reflect the fact that many failed to match his rigorous standards.

In addition, Anglo-Saxon society was a kin-focused world and for the members of one family group to found, own, run, and staff an institution would have been no more than a reflection of the contemporary social mores. Just because Bede depicts them as sewers of vice and sin, it does not necessarily mean they were.

Nevertheless, his criticisms reflect the fact that the cost of diversity is a heterodoxy that can border on corruption. In this instance, diversity meant that noblemen could use the opportunity that church foundation offered to build a nice profitable and commemorative investment for themselves. The monastery could be made in their own image, the abbot (or abbess) being a family member and the community consisting largely of family and retinue who favoured a rest from active life, along with a semi-legal priest or two to make up the numbers.

More importantly, the foundation could be a sensational tax dodge. Endowing a monastery ensured a permanent, hereditary grant of land. As a result, land was secured which would otherwise have reverted in due course to the king for subsequent redistribution. The more monasteries that siphoned land and men out of the Anglo-Saxon economy, the less there would be to fund and protect the land. This was what Bede was nervous about as he completed *Ecclesiastical History*.

The church authorities also recognised the problem. A council in the 740s set out to reform monasteries. Its canons forbade monks and laymen to mix or conduct secular business, condemned drunkenness, ordered prayers for king and laity, and prohibited priests from singing like secular poets. Another, sixty years later, decreed that no monastery was to presume to elect a layman or secular lord 'over Christ's inheritance'. Bishops also sought to eliminate lay lordship by securing reversions to the see or by attempting to oversee abbatial elections. These measures had some success but it was not until the monastic reforms at the end of the tenth century that the problem of over-secular minsters was addressed in any systematic or successful way.

It would be wrong to dismiss minsters out of hand for these failings. We should not take Bede's criticisms too severely. As noted, he had very high standards. More pertinently, as with the foundation of parish churches centuries later, association with lay power did not automatically condemn every religious institution. And legislation is bound to reflect the less successful aspects of minster foundations: just because there was a law prohibiting clerical drunkenness, we should not assume all clerics were drunks.

The important point for our purposes is to note that English minsters were an assorted and complex group. The absence of rigid foundation conditions encouraged diversity and enabled quick growth. The absence of any official monastic rule allowed abbots and abbesses to draw up their own, and shape their foundations in their own image. Remoteness from any bishop or diocesan centre acted as further encouragement for variety and, in any case, royal abbots and abbesses had rather more clout than most bishops.

Under these conditions minsters spread very rapidly and by 800 few settlements in lowland England would have been more than six miles from one. Varied in their origins and idiosyncratic in their organisation, minsters became the ecclesiastical network in Anglo-Saxon

England centuries before the parish system. And they have much to offer twenty-first-century England.

A Pastoral Community

The variety of organisations and absence of any rigid monastic rule meant that the functions of minsters were many and various. The only common theme that unites them all was that they were communal churches.

With the exception of a minority of solitary peripatetic preachers, all ecclesiastics of the Anglo-Saxon age, at least until the first parish churches started appearing at the end, were attached to some form of community. Whether they were concerned primarily with the contemplative or pastoral life, they lived together.

This community feature was reinforced by the fact that communities of any size had more than one church and would be likely to boast a group of ecclesiastical buildings. This was a feature that could be traced back to the classical period when newly state-supported Christianity regularly generated groups of ecclesiastical buildings, with atria, baptisteries, mausolea and martyria surrounding a central church.

Many minsters followed this pattern, although with new buildings accreting round the main church rather than all being built at once. In such a way, the minster community would live in an enclosure where chapels, holy wells, refectories, dormitories, retreat houses and cemeteries would gradually grow up around the original church building. As time went on, larger minsters began to look more like towns than just churches. It should hardly be surprising to learn that many towns – among them what we now call Westminster – actually originated as minster churches. Our traditional image of a monastery, thoroughly isolated from the rest of the world, is particularly out of place here. The minster church would often be the economic centre of an area.

In their variety, density, potential wealth and comparative splendour, larger minsters stood out in a landscape that had only a tiny handful of urban areas. Archaeologists have located on minster sites evidence of cooking, eating, reading, writing, praying, sleeping, teaching, guesthouses and workshops. Only a few minster complexes would have boasted all these but the presence of any would have constituted the only focus in an area, apart from noblemen's halls, which deviated from the agricultural norm. It was for this reason that so many minsters were such rich targets for the Vikings.

Minsters could, therefore, be as 'worldly' as any place in the country, not least because of the aristocratic background and lifestyle of some of their inhabitants. In some ways, many provided the same boost to the local, rural economy, as stately homes were to do a thousand years later, creating opportunities for employment and gathering local settlements around them.

Another reason why a minster might act as a local focus was in its role as the holder of a saint's relics. The Anglo-Saxon world was full of saints, many of whom had very specific local connections. In an age before the Church authorities closely managed the process of canonisation, local dignitaries and holy men and women could find themselves sainted within years of their death. Local legends grew up around them and their relics became of enormous spiritual and economic importance. The miraculous preservation of saints' relics is a common theme in Anglo-Saxon religious records. Their healing power was legendary and attracted hundreds of people. Winchester Minster, we are told, 'was hung all round, from one end to the other on either wall, with crutches and with stools of cripples who had been cured there'.[30] Holy relics and stories of miraculous power were a major attraction. A minster's role in preserving the memory and cult of a local saint and celebrating his or her feast days was also important and helped safeguard local identity and distinctiveness, further marking out a minster as the local centre.

This would not, however, compromise the minsters' more obviously 'spiritual' tasks, which themselves could be as varied as their origins or layout. Thinking about how a minster operated within its environment once again brings us up against anachronistic presuppositions. The later enforcement of strict monastic rules prohibited many monks from engaging in external ministry, although there were a number of exceptions. To the modern mind, a monk's task was one of prayer and study. Conversely, the parish priest had his flock to attend to. Prayer was, of course, an important element in both these lives but corporate, regulated, meditative prayer was a particular call that took the place of the parish priest's pastoral duties.

This strict dichotomy between pastoral and contemplative work is artificial for minster churches. As observed, no minster was completely isolated from lay society and many formed the hub of their local world. There was no law directing monks away from pastoral work and no fundamental incompatibility between being a monk and performing sacramental functions for the laity. Even Bede, the most high-minded of monks in the most 'monastic' of minsters, suggested those in religious life had pastoral responsibilities to the laity.

All Anglo-Saxon ecclesiastics appear to have spent some time in personal, contemplative prayer and in communal worship. In some ways, minsters imitated the family life of the greater cathedrals – houses, at least in theory, of silence and peace, of prayer, reading, study and praise, and, most hopefully, of shunning worldly luxuries. At the same time, however, the various clerics who staffed minster churches had important pastoral duties. These varied from church to church but would include baptising and burying the laity, saying Mass, guarding local holy relics, making intercessory prayer, giving alms, ordering penance, and teaching and preaching the word. On top of these duties, there might also be the social role of providing education and literary services for the landowning classes, and relief to traveller and pilgrim, the destitute and the sick.

Most minsters would have managed only a handful of duties from this list. Indeed, if pastoral care is strictly defined as sacramental duties only, such as baptism, communion and burial, it is likely that a number of minsters would have had an extremely limited pastoral role. If, on the other hand, the definition is widened to include teaching, preaching, caring for the sick and pilgrims, and giving alms, then it is probable that all minsters had important pastoral responsibilities.

There is also evidence that minsters acted as local charity centres. Several stories tell of abbots distributing monastic treasures to townsfolk during hard times, to mitigate the effect of famine on the populace. One Anglo-Saxon translation of the Rule of Benedict placed particular emphasis on the monk's duty to the poor.

This combination of pastoral and contemplative work was intended to act as an example to society. These Anglo-Saxon monks were 'inheritors of that dual tradition ... of the recluse who flees the corruption of the world, and that of the imitator of Christ's life on earth'.[31] As one historian has written:

> The example of charity in the ideal Anglo-Saxon priest
> was to be part of a style of life which in all respects

inspired emulation and spiritual renewal in the lay population ... the aim at this period was evidently not to
make of the local clergy a different caste, set above the
laity by its privileges and avoidance of manual toil – that
would come later – but rather that they should exercise
their pastoral duty, first and foremost, through their personal example of life within lay society.[32]

There were inevitably problems with this dual function,
with roles being blurred on occasion. While one church
council urged priests to learn an honest trade, another
rule forbade priests 'to supplement [their] income[s] by
singing songs in taverns'.[33] There is more than one example of Anglo-Saxon ecclesiastics dying in pub brawls.
Nevertheless, this dual communal/social, contempla-
tive/pastoral role remained intrinsic to church life for
centuries.

Missionary Centres

The conversion of England was, at first, a top-down
process. In a manner quite unlike the spread of
Christianity across the Mediterranean half a millennium
earlier, Anglo-Saxon men and women became
Christians because their kings did. This inevitably made
conversion an ongoing process. It is debatable how
quickly men and women in the field grasped and
believed the fundamental tenets of the Christian faith or
to what extent Anglo-Saxon England was a syncretistic
culture. That the conversion of England continued long
after the Isle of Wight became the last Christian kingdom is not debateable.

This had the effect of turning minsters into missionary
churches, whose task was to educate the people in the faith
just as much as it was to pastor to them or administer the

sacraments. This role was compounded by the fact that minsters had the charge of very large parishes, or *parochiae*, areas considerably larger than those over which parish churches later had authority. *Parochiae* often corresponded to royal or aristocratic estates in the age before these were broken up into smaller, more manageable units. As a result, many villages, even where minsters were most densely packed, would have been the best part of a day's journey from their nearest church.

The resulting model for ministry was missionary as much as it was pastoral. Anglo-Saxon minsters became centres for missionary activity from which small groups ventured out into the nominally Christian but often culturally pagan territory which surrounded them, and preached and ministered from bases established within local settlements, such as stone crosses in villages, some of which are still visible in English churchyards, at which local devotions would be performed. Around 700, one Anglo-Saxon nun, the delightfully named Huneberc of Heidenheim, stated, 'on the estates of the nobles and good men of the Saxon race it is a custom to have a cross, which is dedicated to our Lord and held in great reverence, erected on some prominent spot for the convenience of those who wish to pray daily before it'.[34]

Many of the greatest and most highly regarded Anglo-Saxon ecclesiastics travelled great distances, often in inhospitable and hostile territory to reach remote villages, to preach, baptise and visit the sick, who as Bede revealed to Egbert, were not visited by any other churchmen. In his *Ecclesiastical History* he describes, albeit through slightly rose-tinted spectacles, what would commonly happen and how people responded: 'It was the custom at that time amongst the English people, when a clerk or a priest came into a village, for all to gather together at his command to hear the word.'[35]

This was a model that became associated with Celtic Christians and which proved effective in spreading the gospel through the theoretically Christian nation. Bede, a bastion of Roman orthodoxy, describes their work with approval: 'The priests and the clerics visited the villages for no other reason than to preach, to baptise, to visit the sick, in brief to care for their souls.'[36]

As time progressed and the Church became more settled, the peripatetic lifestyle of Celtic preachers was slowly curtailed. A church council held at Chelsea in 813 placed a ban on the nomadic ministrations of Celtic priests and stated that all clergy, except archbishops, must confine activities within their own diocese or parish.

This was probably not simply an ecclesiastical form of Roman imperialism. It is likely that, after the efforts of the previous century and a half, the wide-ranging nomadic work of the early Celtic missionaries was no longer necessary. Instead, their mobile outlook had been inherited and adapted by the more dominant minsters in the ecclesiastical landscape. Responsible for teaching and preaching in areas nowhere near as vast as Cuthbert's but certainly far larger than the average medieval parish, minster clerics adopted a missionary approach, one major difference being that, because they did not feel the call to self-exile that drove many of the Celtic missionaries, they maintained and participated in their communal church structure and travelled in groups rather than as individuals.

One further aspect of the missionary nature of the minsters was their role as teaching and training centres. Inasmuch as there is any evidence, it shows that where schools existed, they were located at minsters. These would not, of course, have been educational establishments in the modern or even late medieval sense of the word, but rather training grounds for priests and clerics.

The episcopal family at Worcester was regarded, at least in part, as a clergy training school, particularly for those destined to hold responsible office in the Church. Bede envisaged Monkwearmouth-Jarrow and other institutions like it as powerhouses producing an elite pastoral force. Monastic communities were not just pastoral communities that served the needs of their localities; they were also outward-looking missionary centres, in much the same way as modern theological colleges, that provided the resources of training, manpower and prayer through which an area might be helped to understand and accept the Christian faith.

The Faith of the Faithful

Understanding the faith of the faithful in any age is difficult. If writing the history of minsters is a matter of piecing together a fragmentary jigsaw, detailing the lives and faith of those who attended them is the same exercise performed in the dark. Conversion was a complicated affair about which it is difficult to generalise.

When Gregory sent Augustine to England, he told him in one letter to smash idols but convert pagan temples to churches, and in another to destroy pagan temples altogether. At the same time, Augustine told Aethelbert of Kent, once he had been converted, to suppress the worship of idols and destroy shrines. The various contradictory approaches were probably complementary within a wide range of tactics.

Continuing pagan practices are rarely mentioned in existing sources, but this is hardly surprising given that all the documents are Christian and most come from the pen of men as orthodox and unworldly as Bede. The 'Penitential of Theodore', dating from the late-seventh or early eighth century, legislates against pagan practices but does not mention pagan priests and seems to suggest that organised pagan cults did not survive. Burial rights show a decisive change at the time of the conversion: pagan-style burials of clothed men and women interred with grave goods on sites outside settlements ceased in the early eighth century. Burial was a single yet enormously symbolic rite of life. Its rapid Christianisation suggests that these nexus points were converted first and most thoroughly.

The biggest single Christian festival of the year, Easter, was named in English after 'Eostre' who was, according to Bede, a pagan goddess whose feast involved the rising sun and was celebrated at the vernal equinox. The ritual and date may have changed but the name did not. For many early Anglo-Saxon men and women, their new faith may have been largely a matter of the old seasonal festivals changing their form and content.

Early English Christianity was a particularly Anglo-Saxon form of the faith. Like the society of the day, the milieu of Anglo-Saxon Christianity was aristocratic, heroic and bold. Poetry of the time turned Moses and Christ into brave warriors. The twelve apostles became glorious thegns. Old Testament narratives of the conquest of Canaan and of the heroes of Israel were often preferred to the more obviously peaceable teaching of the New Testament.

The faith also attained much local colour. In Celtic areas in particular there was a high proportion of local saints' cults and this localised form of devotion was also important in the Anglo-Saxon kingdoms. Older cultic sites, such as holy wells and cemeteries, often survived within the newly established minster *parochiae*, with minster priests going to them to officiate at baptisms and funerals. Minsters acted as guardians of saints' lives and deeds, celebrating their festivals, tending their tombs, and guarding and distributing their relics. Such cults and feast days were popular with the laity not least because they conferred prestige and attracted pilgrims. It may not be an exaggeration to suggest that the 'continued adherence to Christianity on the part of the laity may well have owed as much if not more to their devotion to saints' cults as to clerical behaviour'.[37]

It would, however, be a mistake to patronise or dismiss Anglo-Saxon Christianity for these habits. Quite apart from the fact that Christianity inevitably adopts, to some degree, the clothes of every age and culture in which it finds itself, there are signs that neither the conversion nor the subsequent Christianisation were as culturally conditioned as might first appear.

In the *Ecclesiastical History* Bede tells a story, through one of King Edwin's advisers, of a sparrow. It is worthy of Paul at the Areopagus in Athens:

> The present life of man, O king, seems to me, in comparison of that time which is unknown to us, is like to the swift flight of a sparrow through the room wherein you sit at supper in winter, with your commanders and ministers, and a good fire in the midst, while the storms of rain and snow prevail abroad; the sparrow, I say, flying in at one door, and immediately out at another, whilst he is within, is safe from the wintry storm; but after a short space of fair weather, he immediately vanishes out of your sight, into the dark winter from which he had emerged. So this life of man appears for a short space, but of what went before, or what is to follow, we are utterly ignorant.[38]

This is good, old-fashioned Christian apologetics – simple, powerful and culturally relevant. More to the point, it is the kind of teaching that, with a few minor changes, is relevant to every culture.

On a more practical level, St Wilfred's conversion of Sussex saw a marked improvement in local fishing techniques. When he first came to Sussex, Wilfred found a kingdom with a highly nominal Christian population, immune to the efforts of a few monks at Bosham to 'convert' them. He also found a kingdom suffering from a long drought and famine, next to a sea full of fish but without the technology to catch them. Wilfred's response was to tie the Sussex fisherman's eel-catching nets together in such a way as to reap a rich harvest when he went out to sea. The people of Sussex were suitably impressed and paid greater heed to Wilfred's more conventional message. Wilfred subsequently converted the people and began to build up Christian communities before returning, five years later, to Northumberland.

Initial conversion was not always nominal. Some Anglo-Saxon kings turned against their powerful cultural foundations and renounced their warrior codes and duties. Upon conversion, King Sigbert of East Anglia abandoned the world for a monastery. His namesake, King Sigbert of Essex, took the gospel to heart and went so far as to forgive an enemy – for which he was murdered. Forgiveness was a dangerous business in a soci-ety driven by blood feud.

The faith of the faithful was, then, a complex, changing affair and not simply a thin frock worn over the habits and mind of the existing culture. Conversion was 'a blend of reasoned argument, political force and material incentive',[39] with the popular faith increasingly heartfelt and understood through the only categories people knew.

We must also be aware that we see the faith of the faithful through the eyes of Bede and other severe, ecclesiastical chroniclers. Their theology and lifestyle was austerely monastic and they commended the rigours of an ascetic observance which has never really appealed to the faithful in any age. There is no reason to doubt Alcuin's complaint that people 'wish to have sacred things round their necks, not in their hearts,'[40] and that 'with these holy words of God or relics of the saints [they] go to their filthy acts'.[41] Yet it would be a mistake to read into this the idea that the new faith was a sham or irrelevance to people.

Even Bede, for whom the laity were in desperate need of guidance, in a sermon preached on Christmas Day emphasised that the term pastor could be applied not only to bishops, priests, deacons, and monasteries, but to any of the faithful who exercised a right custody in his home, however humble.

However one views the faith of the faithful – as a warrior Christianity, a folk faith which mingled Woden with Christ, as a re-branding of certain favourite festivals, as the Christianisation of fundamental rites of passage, or as an entirely new way of looking at the world – the one clear fact is that it was not a quickly accomplished process, limited to the so-called 'age of conversion' in the seventh century. Mission did not end in the Isle of Wight in 686.

Ultimately, to separate missionary and pastoral work is artificial and for a culture which grew into the Christian faith over hundreds of years, somewhat anachronistic. The cleric's duty to travel and seek out the remote places was a both pastoral and a missionary duty. The inhabitants of Anglo-Saxon England required ongoing education. Long-established pagan cultic activity such as incantation, divination, making vows at trees, keeping Thursdays in honour of Thor, or celebrating 1 January and pagan observances, had deep roots. Bede, with his demanding views on penance, sex and a host of other issues may have felt this need for education particularly intensely, but even putting his high monastic standards aside, the English of his day would have struggled with the understanding and practice of their faith, just as millions have done throughout history. To that extent, the minster church was an institution fitted to its age.

Minster Churches – A Brief Conclusion

Minster churches dominated Anglo-Saxon England long before parishes did. Towards the end of the first millennium, as royal estates fragmented, minster *parochiae* were also broken up. Patronal churches sprang up and assumed many of the minster's roles.

Minsters became increasingly redundant in a land of smaller estates and local churches. The minster system did not die away immediately, of course, and relics of it lasted for centuries. Minster churches often became superior parish churches. Smaller, newer foundations were often subordinated to them, required to pay a token tribute and obliged to attend patronal festivals. Nevertheless, the essential raison d'être of minster churches was gone.

The nation had been Christian for many generations and while pagan practices lived on, people had a far better grasp of the tenets and implications of their faith than their forefathers had when minsters first appeared. Two centuries of Viking raids had severely weakened the system, with the large, wealthy churches providing particularly rich pickings for the raiders. The vigorous religious reforms of the tenth century tore apart the marriage of pastoral and contemplative life that had given minster churches their unique role. From then onwards, at least until the arrival of mendicant friars, as a cleric you devoted yourself to a life of prayer in a monastery, ordered by strict rule and routine, or you had a specifically pastoral role, and worked in and for a village, or more accurately, a village lord. You could not do both.

The unique characteristics of the minster church – its combination of communal life, pastoral activity, missionary work, local focus, educational function and economic importance – became ill suited to later medieval England. Yet, because of the social changes that have shaped Britain over the last century or so, it is just those characteristics that may result in the return of the minster church.

Further Reading

John Blair and Richard Sharpe (eds.), *Pastoral Care Before the Parish* (Leicester: Leicester University Press, 1992)

James Campbell (ed.), *The Anglo-Saxons* (Harmondsworth: Penguin, 1991)

James Campbell, *Essays in Anglo-Saxon History* (London: Hambledon Press, 1986)

John Godfrey, *The English Parish* (London: SPCK, 1969)

4

The Return to Minster Churches

Social Reasons

There are essentially three reasons why minster churches might be the future for the English parish – social, ecclesiastical and historical. Divisions between these are to some extent artificial. Ecclesiastical pressures are often due to social trends, and these trends and the direction of history are, of course, intimately related. Never-the-less, looking at each separately helps clarify the issues of population, pastors and processes that make our twenty-first century culture open to an eighth-century solution.

Twenty-first and eighth-century Britain are, of course, unrecognisably different in almost every respect and there can be no question of imitating precisely all the details of the Anglo-Saxon minster system when planning the future of the English parish. However, many of the trends which shape our lives today, such as the widespread loss of a sense of place, our consumerist expectations or the missionary field that Britain has become, are better suited to a minster approach than the modified if still medieval one we have today.

What follows in this chapter is not an attempt to detail all modern British social trends or even an attempt to chart those relevant to the Church. Instead, the chapter simply takes a handful of issues which are particularly relevant to the way the Church structures itself and suggests that, while we can and have adapted the parish system to deal with them, a minster approach might be more effective.

Our Changing Sense of Place

Describing her childhood in the north Oxfordshire hamlet of Lark Rise in the 1880s, Flora Thompson wrote, 'horizons were widening; a stranger from a village five miles away was no longer looked upon as "a furriner"'.[42]

These days, the idea of horizons widening to beyond five miles is almost incredible. Most people have friends and relatives scattered across the country or even the world. We tend to share our streets with strangers and find ourselves travelling to see our friends and companions more than ever before. Lark Rise was backward even then but Flora Thompson's comments highlight one of the biggest changes of the twentieth century: the way we relate to place.

The figures speak for themselves. As a nation we travel over three times further today than we did in 1952. We travel further – to work, to school, to the shops and to visit friends – than we used to. The average person makes over a thousand journeys per year, totalling nearly 7,000 miles, 2,000 miles more than in 1975. This is forecast to double again in the next twenty-five years. We also move house more frequently than we used to, with nearly half of the British population moving in the 1990s. By 2001 there were nearly 1.5 million housing transactions per year. We have become a nation always on the move.

The consequences of this are complex. On the positive side, our mobility has powered economic growth as labour shifted to fit the market gaps. It has offered individuals previously undreamt-of possibilities: no longer are young men and women confined to a future defined by their parent's trade, address, class, or religious denomination. It has also helped address social claustrophobia and challenge cultural myopia, as we become more familiar with other cultures and worldviews and less wary of them.

But the changes have not been exclusively positive and we are beginning to realise that the social costs can outweigh the personal and economic benefits. People today spend far more time in their cars, away from their neighbourhoods, leaving less time to form meaningful relationships with the people in the neighbourhood. This has weakened communities and left us in a world that seems full of strangers. Families have also been weakened as the culture of job mobility, compounded by a time-consuming commute, has reduced family interaction time.

As communities are weakened and local neighbourhoods become anonymous, fluid and increasingly empty, crime increases. In a world full of strangers, it is infinitely easier for criminals to blend in. This in itself can provoke fears over the invisible enemy 'out there' and, somewhat ironically, lead people to demonise groups in a way in which the traditionally static community is thought to do.

Mobility also creates a dispersed society. Residential developments expand around towns, retailers relocate out of town and offices move to business parks. The resulting suburban sprawl inclines people to drive everywhere. Local retailers, unable to match the convenience (and price) of out-of-town superstores, find it difficult to survive and town centres are starved of their individuality, colonised by identical chain stores or abandoned as economically unviable.

Much of this is the worst case scenario but, even so, it still points to the fact that our 'hypermobile' culture cannot continue without some very important values being sacrificed. We need to balance the freedom that our mobility offers us with the sense of community, belonging and security that it subtly erodes.

Whichever road we choose (and all current indicators point towards it being the former), our changing sense of place is something the Church needs to recognise. Put bluntly, when the population's everyday horizons have broadened so much, the Church should not try to live in small, outdated, irrelevant, largely artificial administrative postal squares. It needs to operate on a larger scale.

Parish boundaries mean very little to today's parishioners, and have done so since the last rogation walks were recorded in the eighteenth century. They are effectively little more than legal boundaries, which serve to isolate clergy and congregations, and irritate non-Christians who find their desire to marry in an attractive church is not as easily realised as they wish. Anglican Christians cross boundaries with little compunction and many churches have over half of their electoral role living outside the parish. In fact, these days we *naturally* live and operate in *parochiae* rather than parishes. Our natural form of transport is the car, which we use indiscriminately for shopping, leisure, work and school. In 1998 the average person travelled 6,800 miles a year (excluding air travel); 5,590 miles were by car. In 1999 the averages for the various journeys we made were: commuting to work, 8.1 miles; the school run, 2 miles; shopping, 4 miles; and leisure, 8½ miles. Overall, for all journeys, the average was 6½ miles, which was nearly a third as much again as it was in 1975.

There is much to say for the idea that this is one area in which the Church of England can be truly counter-cultural through being committed to a locality and by helping rebuild the community, which our love of mobility seems intent on ignoring or destroying. However, it can do this without sticking religiously to the parish model. The parish may epitomise the embodied community and this principle should be recognised, but the principle can be retained without preserving its precise and constricting geographical limitations. Minster churches were territorial. Minster clergy regularly travelled, ministered and evangelised among local communities. Conversely people from local communities would travel to the minster church when necessary. Just because it was only the later parish system which could boast that 'every blade of grass' was covered, that does not mean minsters were not territorially concerned.

One of the best estimates for the average distance between a settlement and a minster by 800 AD – six miles – chimes almost exactly with the average journey distance in Britain today. This is a neat parallel but the precise distances are largely irrelevant. What the Church needs to do is to strike the balance between acting as a rooted community and recognising people's broadened geographical horizons. The minster system, with its dual perspective of the broad minster parish and numerous local Christian communities, reflects this balance.

Local Autonomy

On Sunday 22 September 2002, over 400,000 protestors marched down Whitehall. They comprised The Liberty and Livelihood March, until then the largest public

demonstration in British history. The protest was motivated, at least initially, by the endlessly controversial
topic of hunting, but as people finally marched through
London it incorporated a wide range of rural issues such
as poor public services, disappearing amenities, the crisis in farming, under-investment, the supermarket
stranglehold over the food chain and a vulnerable rural
economy. The unifying factor was the sense that rural
concerns were not of interest to a government too busy
pursuing the interests of comfortably urbanised, middle
England. Town and country were two cultures.

It is wrong to argue that rural areas are necessarily
worse off than urban ones. Research compiled by the
New Policy Institute for the Countryside Agency in 2002
showed that 18 per cent of people in country areas live
in low-income households. This is far too high a figure
by anyone's reckoning but it compares favourably with
24 per cent in urban areas. Moreover, between 1996 and
2001, the number of rural people living on low incomes
fell by around 200,000 to 2.6 million.

A report into Britain's local communities published by
the New Economics Foundation in December 2002
warned that *all* local economies, rural and urban, were in
serious danger of decay. Between 1995 and 2000, the UK
lost a fifth of its 'local' institutions, such as corner shops,
grocers, high street banks, post offices and pubs, and a
further 28,000 were forecast to go over the following five
years. The result, the report concluded would be a ghost
town Britain, with communities and neighbourhoods *in
urban as well as rural areas* losing their economic motors
and so seeing their basic social fabric decay.

The crucial difference is that rural communities, being
more isolated and diffuse, are more vulnerable to the
effect of these trends. As suburban local economies decay,
high streets either become colonised with identikit chain

stores and cut-price outlets, or they completely lose the financial glue which held them together. The prospect of this is grim and often leads to urban decay but population density, proximity to other retail outlets and relative superiority of public transport networks usually mean that if one community decays, a neighbouring one will remain active.

More critically, the weak attachment to place which often characterises urban and suburban areas and the oft-preached importance of a 'vibrant housing market', encourages regular movement so that families and individuals relocate to more amenable areas. None of this justifies the decay of local economies but it does suggest that the effect of local decay in built-up areas is mitigated by other circumstances.

This is not so in rural areas. The farming crisis, low level of rural investment and closure of local outlets make local employment more difficult. The almost complete absence of a public transport network means that without a car it is increasingly difficult to shop or work. The great white hope of broadband internet access often stops at the gates of the countryside, thus threatening to isolate rural areas still further.

A greater sense of local attachment often reduces levels of relocation in the country, making country dwellers less inclined to 'up and off' than their suburban counterparts. And in any case, the ever-growing gap in urban-rural house prices acts as a highly effective barrier to crossing that particular border. One of reasons people do not move from rural Herefordshire to the suburbs of London is because they cannot afford to.

The result is the sense of a deepening divide and impending crisis which drove nearly half a million people to London in September 2002. There are fewer than 12,000 rural shops left in Britain and an estimated 300 close every year. Country pubs in England are shutting at a rate of six a week. Since the 1960s England has lost, to urban sprawl, traffic and light pollution, over 20 per cent of what the Council for the Protection of Rural England calls 'tranquil areas'. The jobless rate for eighteen to twenty-four-year-olds in country areas is more than double that for older workers, encouraging further the rural exodus.

We should rightly recognise in all this that the terms 'rural' and 'urban' are vague themselves. There can be as much difference between a rural community of twenty households and one of 1,000, as there is between the one of 1,000 and suburban sprawl. We should also recognise that the needs of *all* communities are essentially the same – jobs, money, transport, social capital. Nevertheless, the nature of the divide and particular local concerns strongly suggest that a one-size-fits-all approach will not do. And this applies to the Church just as it does the local economy.

Rural churches do have a different role in and relationship to the community than urban or suburban ones. The Vicar of Dibley is a chronic stereotype, trading on all the outmoded and unrealistic generalisations hardened town-dwellers have of the countryside, but somewhere in the depths of its chocolate-box imagery, there lies a kernel of realism.

A parish church will, by necessity, play a different role in a community without any other amenities than it will in a suburb which is crushed under its own weight of pubs, bars, community and leisure centres, shopping arcades, and sports clubs. A church in an isolated and still-defined village will have a different role in a community than one in an area which has rendered all its historic geographic boundaries meaningless. A congregation's, and indeed the broader local community's attachment to a parish church is different in a village with long-standing residents and deep roots than it is in a hypermobile suburb, or even a newly formed 'village'. And all of these will have different functions to the church which has found itself in an urban area frenetic with weekday activity but silent at the weekend.

These differences have in fact existed in Britain, although in a less pronounced form, for centuries. In the Middle Ages, they were reflected in differences between established and long-lived rural parishes and the small, often temporary, street-corner churches which populated towns like Winchester and Norwich. Later on, in the nineteenth century, when the town-country divide became even more pronounced, there were wholly new denominations to reflect the gulf. Different structures of organisation and authority allowed nonconformist chapels to colonise the urban landscape in a way their established counterparts never did, once again reflecting the town-country divide. If the ecclesiastical landscape today reflects this division, it does so only accidentally. If anything, the ubiquitous parish structure actively disregards it.

The clear advantage of the minster system, and what recommends it to the current situation where the urban-suburban-semi-rural-rural spectrum is so broad, is its diversity and flexibility. More by a lack of planning than anything else, a parish-like one-size-fits-all approach was eschewed in the seventh, eighth and ninth centuries, with minsters taking the form required of them by their locality or by the motivations of their proprietor and collegiate staff. They varied from the vast and orthodox foundations such as which Bede inhabited, to the smaller and rather more unorthodox ones which he criticized.

The Church in twenty-first-century Britain can easily throw off the shackles of a single parochial model for the whole country without also abandoning theological unity; maintaining the episcopal structure should ensure this. The understandable concern for theological unity should not be allowed to become a geographical strait-jacket. The closer to ground level we go, the more fluid and locally owned the structures should be. A greater degree of local autonomy would not simply recognise the very real differences between localities, but it would make local knowledge and commitment foundational to the running and very existence of a local church.

A Missionary Outlook

Exactly how far is Britain a post-Christian nation? The answer is critical in determining what shape the Church should be in the twenty-first century, but is also highly dependant on the type of measurement used.

The most commonly quoted and theoretically most reliable figure is that of Sunday church attendance. By that reckoning the answer is undoubtedly 'totally'. Church attendance has been falling steadily since the 1930s when it peaked at around ten million weekly attendees. Church attendance patterns have been changing over recent decades, with more and more people attending fortnightly or less frequently, but irrespective of this, on any realistic calculation, fewer than one in ten people could be seriously classified as 'churchgoers'.

There is more to Christianity than churchgoing, however. Average weekly attendance may provide the best single indicator of the state of the Christian faith of a nation, but its black and white nature paints an overly simplistic picture. When MORI asked people about their religious affiliation throughout the 1990s, the percentage of people who answered 'none' increased from 13 per cent to 18 per cent but was still dwarfed by the 80 per cent who said they had a religion, which for the vast majority was Christianity. More recently and more robustly, the 2001 National Census reported that 71 per cent of people in England and Wales, or 37.3 million people, still claim to be Christian, with only 15 per cent preferring to say they have no religion.

If self-designation complicates the picture, people's attitude to God is even more complex. The 1998 Office for National Statistics Social Trends Survey looked at people's belief in God: 21 per cent of respondents agreed with the statement 'I know God really exists and I have no doubt about it' and 23 per cent with 'While I have doubts, I feel that I do believe in God.' A further 28 per cent were split equally between two statements of more hesitant belief, 'I find myself believing in God some of the time, but not at others', and 'I don't believe in a personal God, but I do believe in a Higher Power of some kind.' Overall only one in ten people surveyed agreed with the simple statement 'I don't believe in God.' A post-Christian nation is not necessarily a post-theistic one.

Britain, then, is at least as nominally Christian as it is post-Christian. Established religions do not exist in a vacuum, however, and recent decades have shown an upsurge in 'spirituality'. Between 1987 and 1999 the percentage of people who said they were aware of some kind of spiritual experience in their lives increased from 48 per cent to 76 per cent. In research conducted by the University of Nottingham in 2000, David Hay and Kate Hunt found that, in spite of a reluctance to talk about spirituality, and a default position which meant they had to criticise religious institutions in public, people with no active churchgoing habits were willing to consider themselves spiritual. They may have been embarrassed to talk about such matters, devoid of any common, reliable vocabulary on which to draw, and inclined to construct their own theology using fragments of Christian and other worldviews, but they were still acutely conscious of 'something there'.

As with the 'bums on seats' data, however, this information has its problems. Just because people say they are spiritual it does not mean they are, or that it influences their life in any way. In many ways, spirituality has become the latest, chicest consumer accessory in a marketplace that is more and more post-material (at least according to some commentators). It is often paraded as a badge to show how well rounded, sophisticated and sensitive someone is as an individual. Spirituality may be a bridge to Christianity but the two are by no means synonymous. People who consider themselves spiritual are quite happy (without actually knowing what they are talking about) to dismiss biblical historicity or criticise biblical morality as recent research has shown.

The answer to the posed question, then, is varied. We do not go to church. We distrust institutions. We damn religions. We are irreducibly spiritual but our spirituality is a vague and malleable concept. We know next to nothing about Christianity, but know enough to dismiss it. Yet, ultimately, most of us like to call ourselves Christians. Whether this actually leaves us a post-, pseudo- or sub-Christian nation will depend on our use of those definitions. The one safe conclusion is that we are not a Christian nation and need to hear the gospel afresh.

And this comprises a third 'social' reason why minster churches are suited to modern Britain. Minsters, unlike their parochial successors, were primarily evangelistic in outlook. They were essentially missionary churches. England, superficially Christian by the last decade of the seventh century, was in reality anything but, and the evangelism of the nation continued for at least a century more. Anglo-Saxon men and women may have been baptised and buried according to Christian rites, celebrated Christian festivals and maintained the tradition of local Christian saints, but their basic knowledge of the implications of the gospel is likely to have been shaky, not least because it was so antipathetic to their own warrior culture.

Either way, the similarity between early Anglo-Saxons and twenty-first-century Britons is striking. Both are nominally Christian. Both have a vague knowledge of the faith. Both recognise and celebrate the major festivals, although both confuse them with popular misconceptions and elements of folkloric-influenced spirituality. Both have a greater need for mission than they do for pastoral work, although it should be emphasised that the distinction between the two is not always that clear.

There are, of course, differences, not least that Anglo-Saxon society was built on common rite and ritual, and on the respect of authority in a way the modern West most certainly is not. Nevertheless, the future of the English parish needs to be guided by the principle that church centres are resource centres for on-going mission rather than simply bases for local pastoral work. They can still be the latter, of course, but in a structure which has a strong emphasis on, for example, cell groups and every member ministry. The ordained minister and staff team, who would comprise the minster college, would be free to concentrate more on outreach and work in the wider community. Whether that entailed the travelling on foot from village to village that Bede so approved of, or, more probably, putting energy into mission and community services that take the good news of Jesus

Christ into the lives of people who have by and large
dismissed him, will depend on the individual minster
church.

Neutral Space

Public space is not what it used to be. When it opened in
north Kent, in 1999, Bluewater shopping mall was hailed
as a kind of retail nirvana. The place incorporates three
different malls and three distinct 'leisure villages'.
Kentish oast houses and a Kew Garden greenhouse
inspire its architecture. It has seven lakes, fifty acres of
landscaped parkland, forty restaurants, cafes and bars,
320 shops, and 13,000 parking places, together with a
continually changing schedule of events, festivals and
live performances. There is nothing more a modern,
civilised Westerner could want.

Bluewater is unusual only inasmuch as it has been
professionally executed. All over the country public
space is slowly being colonised by commercial interests.
From adverts being projected onto the House of
Commons to roundabouts being sponsored by local
curry houses, fewer and fewer places are free from commercial interests. Public space has been captured by
commerce.

Public advertising is not new, of course. Old high
streets had more than their fair share of advertisements
but these, as John Humphrys observes in his book
Devil's Advocate, took their place amidst the existing
serendipity, rather than dominate the environment
alongside ubiquitous retailers. High streets once included churches, chapels, cinemas, theatres, libraries, town
halls, schools, banks, solicitors' offices, parks, play-
grounds, marketplaces, war memorials, pubs, cafes and
private houses. Modern malls seek to emulate this

variety, but the unavoidable difference is that *then* you were a citizen, walking around a publicly owned district which had no implicit demands of you, whereas *now* you are a consumer in a 'high street' which, in truth, is about nothing more than encouraging you to spend your money. The very act of being has become subordinate to buying.

It is hardly surprising that shopping centres have been called the cathedrals of the new age. The parallels are many. Not only are they the biggest, shiniest, newest buildings in the country, not only do they dominate their localities, not only is money our modern god, not only do we usually attend them on a Sunday, but they are also increasingly places where we are encouraged simply to 'be'.

Contrary to modern opinion, which is usually shaped by the cold, empty, drafty, whitewashed state of many churches today, parish churches would originally also have been places to 'be'. They may not have had quite such an emphasis on spending money – although the naves, which were effectively owned and run by the congregations, might have been used as markets – but they were places where people gathered, because they were the largest, driest, warmest and safest building in most villages.

They would also have been riotously colourful and busy with the records of human life, both past and present, a repository for community memory and identity. Not only did the parish church act as a local community centre and meeting place, but it would also provide storage for communal property such as parish chests and long ladders, and emergency equipment, such as fire extinguishing apparatus. The church and churchyard were the focus for community festivities and, if unintentionally, the local playground too, if the records of windows broken by children's ball games are to be believed.

Whether minster churches served such a function is less clear. On the one hand, their economic importance for the locality, their protection of the local saint's relics and their superiority over the early parish churches would have almost guaranteed a certain 'community centre' function. On the other hand, their distance from some villages would have prevented them from having as vital a community role as later, more immediate parish churches did.

Today, however, small congregations, high maintenance bills, overworked clergy, out-dated and over-protected buildings, and limited space prevent parish churches from fulfilling this role. The need for a neutral space, where people can meet, talk, work, hire rooms, enjoy coffee, have a bite to eat, let children play, etc. – without the implicit but omnipresent message, 'BUY!' – is great, and it is one which newly founded, equipped, collegiate minster churches might just satisfy.

Intimacy and Experience

One of the side effects of the decay of safe, accessible, neutral public space has been the changing nature of the home.

In his influential vision of utopia, *Looking Backward*, written in the 1880s, the journalist Edward Bellamy tells the story of Julian West, a young man who falls into a trance in 1887 and wakes up 113 years later in the new millennium. The America he knew has left behind it the industrial horrors of the nineteenth century and is now 'one great business syndicate . . . employing all citizens, who share equally in its profits'.[43]

Bellamy's vision of utopia, like many written at the time, had an explicit and total faith in the capacity of technology to solve man's problems. At one point, the narrator is introduced to a device of music-by-telephone which carries music played live in certain dedicated music halls to people's houses by means of telephone cables. He is suitably impressed. 'It appears to me,' he remarks, 'that if we could have devised an arrangement for providing everybody with music in their homes ... we should have considered the limit of human felicity already attained, and ceased to strive for further improvements.'[44] The awe with which the narrator assesses this forerunner of the radio is an important reminder that today most Westerners live in a world that a century ago would, materially speaking, have been a vision of paradise.

The inter-war period saw houses electrified, production-line technology spread, hire-purchase agreements become increasingly available, and desire elevated above need as a justification for purchase. Between 1951 and 1973 the British economy grew by nearly 3 per cent per annum. People spent their money on every kind of labour-saving device and entertainment product they could afford (and many they could not). Record players and black-and-white televisions were joined by cassette recorders and colour TVs in the 1970s, video recorders and CDs in the 1980s, and DVDs, PCs, games consoles, and Internet connections in the 1990s.

In the same post-war period, the population increased by 20 per cent and the number of households nearly doubled. The difference in growth levels resulted in the average household size falling from 4.6 people per household in 1900 to 2.4 in 2000. Houses became full of things rather than people.

These changes had two effects on people. The first was that they became harder to impress with spectacles and the second was that their homes became increasingly personalised and isolated places.

This has had an impact on attitudes towards church-going. When you can sit at home in the comfort of your armchair and watch, for example, *The Matrix* on DVD on your 24" widescreen TV, the thought of sitting on a hard, Victorian bench for an hour, rising only to crawl through an excruciatingly slow, off-key rendition of 'All things bright and beautiful', has limited appeal. The comparison may be hyperbolic but the principle remains true. In a world of 'home cinemas', today's attractive, but largely empty, parish churches do not impress in the way they used to.

At one point in *Peasants*, Wladyslaw Reymont's novel of rural life in late nineteenth-century Poland, the ignorant peasant Kuba, an object of ridicule to richer peasants, elbows his way to the front of the congregation during Mass in the village church. His peers are astonished and resentful that he should deem himself worthy of a seat well above his station in life, but Kuba is transfixed by what he experiences and is immune to their indignation:

> On every side, gold shone bright, tapers gleamed, and nosegays of red flowers were flaming. From the walls, from the stained glass windows, austere saintly visages, surrounded with aureoles, bent above him; streams of gold, purple and violet came down, flooding his face and head with rainbow tints ... Dissolved into ecstasies with the joy of the beauty before him, he was too much awed to move, and knelt motionless, gazing at the sweet dark maternal face of the Virgin of Czestochowa, and with parched lips said prayer after prayer, and sang with such force and fervour, welling up from his enraptured heart, that his husky tuneless voice was heard high above the others.[45]

The awesome combination of light, colour, sound, smell, and ritualised movement was pure drama to him, taking him out of himself and giving him a glimpse of paradise. It is easy to forget that this was one of the primary functions of church attendance in the Middle Ages, to transport parishioners just as much as to instruct them.

Today's attractive, but largely empty, old parish churches cannot begin to approach this grand, numinous experience. Instead, it is our worship that can and should transcend the mundane and offer a 'foretaste of heaven'. Such an ambition has been fundamental since the dedication of Solomon's temple and has a long history within Christendom, and while there is no direct correlation between big churches and the quality of the worship, the fact remains that a paucity of people and resources on the ground often justifies outsider criticism of church being 'boring'. A message about joy, celebration, glory and hope, about the unity of all people, about the transcendent breaking in to the immediate, about light cutting through darkness, merits a bit of 'theatre'. Most churches aspire to this but the truth is that through no fault of their own, most do not have the resources of money, time, energy and space to achieve it. Pooling resources might make a different story.

At the other end of the scale, there is the issue of people and their homes. The strength of the minster system is that it does not simply fall into the mistake of believing big is beautiful. The minster was not the *only* form of church but, as observed, acted as a resource centre, educating and equipping villages and hamlets in its district. There was an emphatically local element to the system.

That local element did not, at least at first, consist of independent church buildings, but rather of the Christian community meeting in the open air, at a village cross or in existing buildings. Whatever the precise arrangements were, they remind us that the Church can exist without churches and suggest that the minster system might dovetail neatly with local, cell or house congregations.

Such local churches offer an intimate and relaxed atmosphere of fellowship which larger congregations, especially large minster ones cannot. They also provide an arena for immediate pastoral support that does not always exist in parish churches and probably would not in minster churches.

A new minster system would offer the opportunity to integrate these two crucial elements: the 'transporting' worship of the 'big' and the intimate fellowship of the 'small'. Both are needed in a population which treats light entertainment as a 'transport of joy' and for whom 'intimacy' has become all but synonymous with 'sex'.

Social Reasons – A Brief Conclusion

These, then, are a handful of social reasons why a minster system would be better suited to modern Britain than a parish one. Our sense of place has changed and we naturally operate in minster districts in our everyday life, shopping for churches and crossing parish boundaries with ease.

Minster churches were primarily mission-orientated in outlook, offering a much-needed approach in our peculiarly post-Christian nation. They could also offer the opportunity for people to enjoy neutral space for everyday interactions and relationships, as well as the pooled resources for truly transcendent worship. At the same time, the minster system demands a local church movement in which more intimate, pastoral concerns would be dealt with.

The truth is that each of these reasons could be ignored and many churches would continue doing excellent work in their communities. They are reasons for change which offer opportunities for the future. Opportunities, if ignored, will not cripple the Church but might well slow it down and present for it a bleak future in which it eventually runs out of steam.

The implicit threat behind the social reasons for adopting a minster system is, therefore, one of a long, drawn-out death. The threat behind the ecclesiastical reasons is rather more brutal.

Further Reading

Michael Moynagh, *Changing World, Changing Church* (Monarch, 2001)

5

The Return to Minster Churches

Ecclesiastical Reasons

The ecclesiastical reasons for moving from a parish to a minster system are fewer but rather more pressing. In effect, they boil down to three key issues: clergy, churches and congregations.

Clergy

The 'clergy situation' within the Church of England at the turn of the twenty-first century does not look promising. The declining number of ordained ministers and ordinands is making a universal parish system increasingly difficult to maintain. In spite of a massive influx in the 1990s through the ordination of women, the current number of around 8,700 clergy does not sit easily with the need to staff 13,000 parishes and 16,000 churches.

Financial problems add to this. After the much-publicised loss of £800 million in the early 1990s, an estimated £400 million was also lost in the first years of the following decade. The current fund of around £3.5 billion may have performed consistently well throughout the 1990s, but the Church's responsibility for its retired clergy and its enormously expensive building fabric mean that the fund is simply not enough. Somewhat ironically, the fall in active clergy is actually beneficial. The Church could not afford one vicar per parish, even if there were the men and women to fill the vacancies.

The obvious solution to declining funds is an increase in parishioners' giving. This has occurred and is slowly changing the situation. Nevertheless, despite bishops voting for a 16.5 per cent pay rise for clergy in November 2002, the fact remains that the clergy are still underpaid for their professional status and the hours they put in.

It is widely recognised, however, that clergymen and women do not do the job for money. A 2001 survey found that although only one in ten clerics were satisfied with the level of their stipend and around a third were in debt, this was not a cause for low job satisfaction. Instead, low morale results from overwork, vulnerability and a sense of isolation.

Overwork is an issue across the board but is particularly a problem for rural clergy who find themselves in charge of a growing number of parishes simply because there is not the manpower or financial resources to replace neighbouring retiring clergy. As the Archbishop of York said on a Radio 4 programme in November 2002:

> The parish system itself is in very great danger of breaking down almost altogether and one of my concerns of the present time is the fact that, certainly in our own diocese of York, we're looking at adding on [parishes]. Will a vicar, who's already got three parishes, take on another and then another and another? … We really cannot go on like that.[46]

Vulnerability is, conversely, more of an issue in urban and suburban parishes. A survey commissioned by the Home Office and conducted by the Royal Holloway Research Department of the University of London in 2001 showed that threats and abuse were helping to create a climate of fear among clergy. One in eight of the Anglican clergy interviewed had been physically assaulted at some point over the previous twenty-four months; one in five had been threatened with harm; seven out of ten had been sworn or shouted at; and 39 per cent of male clerics and 51 per cent of females said they were afraid of becoming a victim of violence during their work.

Although a sense of vulnerability was detectable in all areas, the report found that clergy working in the inner cities were more likely to report that they had been threatened than those working in rural areas. The problem was not, however, simply limited to poverty-stricken, run-down urban estates. One major source of violence came from 'middle-class parishioners who were abusive at the very least if they could not get their way with regard to making arrangements for baptisms or weddings'.

The sense of isolation is far more vague and has nothing like as obvious an impact on clergy lives as over-work or violence. In one sense, the priesthood can be the least isolated of all careers, with pastoral work and church 'management' plunging an incumbent into an often choppy sea of people. The time for personal prayer, study and sermon preparation does not so much isolate as offer a time to reflect and gain perspective, something which most people would benefit from today.

Yet clerics can easily become isolated from their peers and others who might offer pastoral support, moral counselling, intellectual stimulation, management advice and spiritual succour. If one's role is heavily based on dispensing grace and advice, time and a source of real rest and replenishment is needed. The parish incumbent's autonomy, authority and independence all mitigate against this. It is possible to become very lonely even when immersed in people eighteen hours a day.

A minster model would not 'solve' any of these problems, but it would provide a basis from which they might be dealt with more successfully. A fundamental aspect of minster churches was their collegiate structure, a feature that would do much to counter the natural barriers set up by the parish system and also help address the danger of overwork. The emphasis on shared ministry would offer, indeed make mandatory, the on-going support, teaching, counselling, encouragement and guidance which are all much needed among clergymen and women today.

The collegiate system could also extend beyond ordained ministers and provide the opportunity for a significant level of lay participation. The days when ordained ministers ran churches single-handedly are long gone and although there is growing recognition of the importance of serious lay responsibility (not to mention a pressing need for it) the current parochial structure makes lay participation very difficult in anything but an ad hoc, unpaid, semi-official way.

A collegiate system would extend the support, teaching and encouragement beyond the clergy to incorporate lay members who wish to contribute to church life in a more organised, professional and directed way. This would do nothing to change the existing hours of a congregation's ad hoc involvement, but it would give the opportunity for those emerging from school, university or their working life, and those who wish to donate a day or two of their working week to their church, to contribute in a organised, structured and valuable way. In

such a way, minster churches would act as small-scale,
hands-on training centres, much in the same way Bede
envisaged they might in the eighth century.

One further, major advantage of the minster system
for clergy is that it offers a much greater opportunity for
specialisation than exists at the moment. The current
parochial system requires vicars and, to a lesser extent,
curates to be all things to all men, women and children.
The call for baptism, marriage, burial, pastoral work,
teaching, preaching, hospital visiting, evangelism, management, strategy and much else besides is unceasing.
Few ministers are equally talented in all of these roles,
and in truth, few, if any, are capable of discharging all
such duties even to their own satisfaction. Everyone has
his or her own particular talents and it is a poor use of
resources when individuals are required to do a little bit
of everything every now and then, rather than concentrate on that which they do best. The body is not, after
all, made up of one part, but of many.

A minster model, with its extensive parish and large,
flexible, central collegiate minster church (or possibly
churches) would give the chance for particular ministers
to specialise, for example, in marriage (and marriage
courses), funerals (and subsequent pastoral visits),
infant baptisms (and the potential for education and
pastoral support they might offer), evangelism courses,
outreach work, pastoral work among the elderly, youth
work and overall strategy planning.

Specialisation within a collegiate system would not
mean that clergy avoid things they either dislike or feel
less than perfectly able to perform: as ways of learning
and developing, challenging tasks can rarely be bet-
tered. Instead, it would encourage the optimal use of
resources. Moreover, a minster system would also create
ways in which churches of different worship styles and

(dare I say it) theologies might work alongside one another. Instead of parish churches being even more isolated than they already are because they have a slightly different theology to neighbouring churches, a minster parish would, in a sense, reflect the Anglican communion in miniature,* with each minster parish having areas of liberal, Anglo-Catholic or evangelical theology, or charismatic or traditional worship.

In spite of how it may sound, there is no naïvety in this suggestion. Christians have proved to be masters of sectarianism in the past and living proof of the aphorism that civil wars are the bitterest. The thought of working closely, let alone belonging together in the same minster parish, will have some vicars and congregations choking in horror. Love, joy, peace, patience, kindness, goodness, faithfulness, gentleness and self-control seem to go right out of the window if my neighbour has a slightly different attitude to the Eucharist or to human sexuality than I do.

Similarly, there is much truth in the idea that clergy, because of the existing parish structure, are trained for leadership and independence more than they are for fellowship and cooperation. As one expert in rural ministry has said, 'Theological colleges still think in terms of the all-powerful incumbent. They do not teach clergy to relate to one another, which is why you get these frightful rows in cathedral closes.'

This is no place to venture into the troubled territory of theological disputes except to say that advocating broad, flexible, locally determined, inclusive minster parishes is not done without recognising the problems

---

* This paragraph was written before the turbulant summer of 2003 and in the (naïve?) optimism that there would still be an Anglican communion to reflect.

and challenges they will present and acknowledging that structural change will only ever be cosmetic if it is not accompanied by the appropriate changes in training, outlook and fellowship. Put more frankly, if the Anglican Christians cannot learn to live in harmony and peace together, they do not deserve to be – and probably will not remain – the bearers of Christ's message in England.

Churches

The Anglican Church, after having been known for generations as the Tory party at prayer, is fast becoming the National Trust at prayer. Simon Jenkins' summary of English churches is just about right. Parish churches are, first and foremost, architectural, artistic, historical, local gems. They need restorers rather than rectors.

The scale of the challenge is enormous. The Church has legal responsibility for 16,000 parish churches, of which around 11,000 are listed – the vast majority of which are Grade I (of exceptional interest) or Grade II* (particularly important buildings of more than special interest). In some counties, four in every five Anglican churches are listed. The denomination with the next highest number of listed buildings is Methodism, with around 600. Altogether, parish churches and cathedrals account for over 31 per cent of all Grade I listed buildings in Britain.

The cost of maintaining and repairing buildings is vast. One recent estimate put it at £120 million per year, of which the Church pays around £110 million, the rest coming from English Heritage and lottery funded schemes. Over the last thirty years, around 900 churches have been turned to other uses (such as arts venues, craft workshops, housing and offices), raising over £31 million, of which more than £25 million has been ploughed back into diocesan work. Nevertheless, in the overall scheme of things, this has not done much more than scratch the surface.

Some caveats need to be made at this point. Old does not automatically mean bad. It is easy to get carried away in enthusiasm for the future and forget that the past can be an ally rather than a foe. In spite of only seeing around one million people attending on an average Sunday, the Established Church has a vast fringe constituency. Whether this is determined by the million or so extra who attend at Easter, the two million extra at Christmas, or the thirty million more who, despite the complete breakdown of any social pressure to do so, still choose to call themselves Christians, there is still a large and valuable residue of good feeling and much contact. No one is under any illusion that *calling* oneself an Anglican actually has any impact whatsoever on one's beliefs and behaviour (research shows that it does not) but the fact still remains that for these people, the parish church is in the bloodstream, a place to turn to, if only occasionally, for help, peace or perspective. In different ways, cathedral attendance in the wake of 11 September 2001 and parish church attendance in Soham, after the murder of two schoolgirls in the summer of 2002, both reflected this.

On top of this, the role of a parish church in certain areas is altogether more central to the community than in others. As one team minister told me, old churches can be a very *positive* thing: they can be symbols of faith within a community, even for non-churchgoers; they may be vital centres of local identity; and, even in the midst of awkward and insatiable demand for restoration, they can be a means through which the Christian faith and a sense of community is stubbornly brought into reality. Problems *can* be their own solutions.

The retort to reforming zeal is, then, quite clear: the Church abandons its heritage at a great risk. Yet, recognising that the argument has two cogent sides should not preclude some form of judgement. It may be true that, as the commentator Andrew Brown said on the Radio 4 programme, *Analysis*, 'a Church that gives up on its beautiful buildings is also giving up a great deal of what makes it attractive to outsiders', but the truth is that a Church whose main attraction to 'outsiders' is its beautiful buildings is not a Church at all.

It is also true that proposals to alter churches that are three-quarters empty on an average Sunday are often met with howls of protest from 'parishioners' whose only contact with the building is every other Christmas. If that is the case, and if the local community does value its church so much, it *must* take active responsibility for it. If the nation wants churches as heritage sites, it should pay for them, as already happens in France. With the right of enjoyment, comes the responsibility of upkeep.

For the minster church system to have a real future in the twenty-first century, it has to wade into this particularly awkward and often bloody battlefield. It does so, however, with a helpfully flexible and nuanced approach. On the one hand, it is clear that the kingdom of God is about hearts not stones. If money, time and energy are being exhausted on what is essentially heritage upkeep, something must change. If stone fetters are being placed on local congregations by a wider community which wants to maintain the medieval parish church for the sake of local pride, a confrontation beckons. If a church becomes a museum, it must stop being a church.

On the other hand, the minster system *does not* advocate local withdrawal and/or some form of relentless ecclesiastical centralisation. Essential to the whole system is the idea of a local congregation. Indeed, one of the fundamental objectives for the collegiate minster church is to *serve and equip* the local church, rather than replace or remove it from its locality. It is perfectly possible for the local congregation to remain in the local parish church, and for the local parish church to remain central to the local community, while being connected to and equipped by their minster church.

Whether there is a 'heritage confrontation' or a constructive reshaping of the local church's function will depend largely on local criteria (another reason why the minster system's emphasis on local autonomy is so important). Irrespective of what happens, the minster system does encourage a different approach and outlook. Local church congregations need not just think of themselves as parishioners of their exquisite but uncomfortable, impracticable and expensive Norman church, which they must maintain at all costs for the sake of the Christmas congregation and weekend tourists. Instead, they would think of themselves as parishioners of the local minster church, alongside all their other neighbouring 'parishes', at which they will meet at some point during the month, and from which they can draw support for their various midweek and Sunday at the 'local' church.

Congregations

Just as we need to stop ourselves thinking that, in terms of buildings, old means useless, so we need to realise that for congregations, small does not mean inferior. The average Anglican church today has around fifty adult members in its congregation and ten children. This is lower than any other denomination. On average, Baptist churches have around 115 members per congregation, New churches 138 and Catholic churches 325.

The correlation between size and growth/decline is not, however, straightforward. The denominations that have shrunk most rapidly over the last twenty years are the Anglican, with comparatively small churches, and the Catholic, with unquestionably the largest. Within the Church of England, it is the smallest (i.e. under ten), and the largest (i.e. over 500) congregations that have shown signs of growth over the last decade. In between, there have been many more declining churches than growing ones. Small does not automatically mean failing and it can mean the opposite.

Even with this taster of the complexity of the size issue, one can begin to see that no simple equation will explain the variety of phenomena witnessed. There is the weakening of the cultural attachment to Roman Catholicism, that once slowed decline in that denomination in the twentieth century. There is the profound anti-institutionalism in contemporary culture, that almost certainly affects the most institutional denomination, the established one. There is the imbalance between resources and buildings, that crushed so many Methodist congregations in the early years of the twentieth century and is threatening to do the same to Anglican ones today. Each of these factors will complicate any direct correlation between size and growth, even if such a correlation exists in the first place.

It also appears that a number of 'size' phenomena influence the balance between size and growth. In the 1990s, small congregations often grew not so much because they were small but because being small usually meant other things too. Small congregations often had no resident clergy and were not dependent on a leader. They had to rely on the gifts and shared life of the congregation. It is widely recognised that the more involved people are, the less likely they are to drift away. Participation breeds commitment. Accordingly, belonging mattered more in small churches. In a congregation of ten, someone's absence would always be noticed in a way it would not in a congregation of 200. Proportionally, people matter more in small congregations.

Small congregations were also often based in smaller, rural environments where, as we have already noted, other amenities and services were rapidly disappearing. The congregation, small as it may have been, often attained increased importance within the community simply because the church became the only remaining corporate body in the village and the only remaining incarnation of local identity and solidarity.

These reasons (together with the more prosaic one that it is easier to register statistically significant growth if you are starting from a small base) suggest that it is not so much the small size that facilitates growth but the natural concomitants of being fewer in number – participation, responsibility, belonging, local relevance and loyalty.

Reasons for the decline of larger churches are, predictably, the mirror image of these. A lack of regular commitment, a sense of anonymity, lower levels and need for participation, a reduced sense of belonging and loyalty are all reasons cited by Bob Jackson in his recent analysis of congregation size on growth, *Hope for the Church*. In larger congregations people find it harder to recognise and integrate the newcomer, not least because they are nervous about asking whether someone is actually new. They are also less likely to spot someone's absence and, accordingly, feel resentful themselves at never having been missed. The solution to these problems seems to be, to act small no matter how large you are.

This resolution needs to be modified by other considerations though. Larger congregations may be more vulnerable to decline but it is easy to overlook the fact that they constitute a very significant proportion of the total number of churchgoers. In the UK today, around 50 per cent of Protestant churchgoers attend 15 per cent of the churches with the other half going to the remaining 85 per cent. Although 'thinking small' does have an impact on retention and growth, so does 'thinking big'.

This is a phenomenon long recognised in America, where there is a similar ratio of churchgoers to churches. An article in *Leadership* magazine in 1998 explained it this way:

> A disproportionately large number of the churchgoers born after World War II prefer the very large churches that can respond to their demands for quality, choices and specialised ministries. [A second result of this is] the replacement of the neighbourhood church by the regional megachurch. A third is the rising level of complexity that accompanies this increase in size. A fourth is the growing demand for a high level of competence in the professional staff.

The writer might have added that large churches provide the critical mass that is so vitally important for youth ministry. It can offer massive, uplifting corporate worship. It can afford facilities that smaller churches often cannot, such as crèches, kitchens, cafés, restaurants, games rooms, etc. It is more likely to have the resources of time, money and expertise to develop valuable services, such as a website, a holiday club, schools ministry, mums and toddlers club, or a drop-in centre, not to mention other, more esoteric ones, like drama workshops, music training and fitness clubs. 'Megachurches' can, in other words, build a comprehensive kingdom in a way that smaller ones, through no reason other than their size and its attendant limitations on resources, cannot.

The ideal solution, therefore, is mixed. On the one hand, the need to 'think small' appears to be important inasmuch as it fosters participation, responsibility and a sense of belonging. On the other, thinking big is important inasmuch as it enables congregations to offer services, develop potential and make relationships in a way that small churches are unable to.

The minster church system is flexible enough to accommodate this varying requirement. At its heart is the minster (or 'mega-') church, a heart for the extended locality and a resource centre for other congregations. But equally important is its emphasis on the local congregation, linked very closely, indeed 'belonging' to and within the minster parish but still to some degree independent. The precise balance between these two elements will depend on locality and details but, at the risk of repeating myself, it is exactly this local flexibility that is central to the minster system.

Ecclesiastical Reasons – A Brief Conclusion

These, then, are the ecclesiastical reasons why the Anglican Church should adopt its pre-parochial pastoral and evangelistic model for the twenty-first century. There is also a coda to these particular reasons in the important issue of ecumenism. It should not be beyond the realms of possibility for the minster churches of the twenty-first century to become foundations for local ecumenical partnerships (LEPs).

This book has steered away from the topic of ecumenism in Britain today because, even though it is an important and potentially fruitful area, to deal with it would complicate an idea that, at this early stage, requires the merits of simplicity to find its roots. Nevertheless, it is worth mentioning that LEPs have provided the most tangible success of post-war ecumenism in Britain, especially in the way different denominations have worked together to found churches in new areas. Of course, the logistical and theological problems that would face an inter-denominational minster parish are truly awesome (another reason for not trying to deal with them in such a short book). Nevertheless, if the ecumenical movement has a future in this country – and I believe that it does and must – a revised parochial structure could offer a real opportunity for progress.

Whether minster churches are ecumenical or not, nobody should be under the illusion that developing them would be an easy or straightforward transition. Conservatism, both inside and outside the Church, will be highly resistant to the change. There are significant personal, practical, legal and logistical reasons to impede the idea.

In spite of these, however, the social and ecclesiastical recommendations for it are immense. Recognising these should help overcome the barriers the minster church model will face. Moreover, the idea's greatest strength – that it is historically authentic, older and, ironically, more ecclesiastical in origin than the parish system we have come to know and love – should further help the colossal English adoration of heritage and historical legitimacy.

And it is from history that the final, and perhaps conclusive, reason for the minster model comes. Put simply, we are heading that way already, whether we like it or not.

Further Reading

Peter Brierley, *The Tide is Running Out* (Christian Research, 2000)

Peter Brierley (ed.), *Religious Trends* Vols. 1–4 (London: Christian Research/Harper Collins, 1999–2003)

Bob Jackson, *Hope for the Church* (London: Church House Publishing, 2002)

6

The Return to Minster Churches

Historical Reasons

Before the First World War

In one sense, minster churches never completely disappeared.

As the parish system evolved after the Norman Conquest, minsters became 'superior' or 'mother' churches, often retaining something of their seniority in particular rights. In the early stages mother churches were owed tithe by local chapels, whose congregations were expected to attend at special festivals. Mother churches also often retained the licence for a cemetery and/or font, although these eventually passed into the keeping of parish churches. Even after all these privileges had disappeared, there were still some churches that retained an amorphous sense of seniority and superiority. They were larger, grander, wealthier, or simply tacitly acknowledged as the major church within a defined area.

Centuries later, after the Act of Toleration but before the Methodist revival, a very informal quasi-minster system began to appear through the work of the Old Dissenters. The parish structure was still very much in place as, even after the Act of Toleration, few nonconformist chapels were actually erected. Those that were served almost as latter-day minster churches, providing bases in cities and market towns from which nonconformist ministers travelled to their scattered flock.

During the early nineteenth century, when the Established Church was beginning to face up to the challenge of dealing with the growing and shifting population, one of the arguments which surfaced was that the best way to minister to a changing England was not 'to spread butter thinly but to concentrate it'. Some Anglicans protested that the system of division into many weak units was an error and that a vast parish with ten priests was better than the same area divided into ten districts, each with one priest. Parishes should not be scattered across newly populated areas in small, segregated, isolated units staffed by single, lonely, pressurised clergymen but rather concentrated in larger, better equipped areas, which would minister through a series of pastoral networks which linked the vicar with his congregation.

This was actually seen in a few examples, the most famous of which was in Leeds. Walter Hook was Vicar of Leeds in the early nineteenth century and became for many Anglicans the ideal of a town pastor. When asked how a vicar might cope with such a large and populous parish as his, Hook advised that he should hire a curate who should go out and persuade laymen to help them. The vicar should not tell the curate or the lay workers what to do but allow them to use their 'individual genius' to run business as they saw fit. In an age in which the incumbent was expected to do more or less everything, it was a radically unorthodox and un-Anglican thing to do. In its own mild way it was both localised and collegiate.

At around the same time, the Roman Catholic Church in England was transformed, first by the Act of Emancipation and then later by the agricultural disasters in Ireland, which increased the number of Irish Catholic immigrants, particularly to the north-west of the country. The different arrangements in the Catholic Church, which prevented laymen from conducting services or moving outside the official structure and setting up their own church, meant that the spread of Catholic churches was bound to be far more limited than that of the new Anglican churches over the same period. This had the positive effect of producing a smaller number of larger churches that were staffed by colleges of priests who served larger congregations.

The system worked well but only because of the particular circumstances of Roman Catholic practice at the time. Congregations were willing to travel further. It was a sin not to attend Mass and the immigrant Irish found in church a link with home and nation as well as more obviously spiritual succour. Again, by accident rather than design, a quasi-minster system had been adopted.

In spite of some fears that the Catholic Church was spreading too widely and too quickly, it was not until the twentieth century that real minster-like proposals were taken seriously by the Established Church. The necessary major shift in thinking only occurred when more and more people began to realise that Britain was now less a Christian nation and more a missionary field.

In 1900, an anonymous writer published a pamphlet entitled *The Organisation of the Church in Large Centres of Population*. This focused especially on the area of St Pancras in London, which was by now extremely densely populated and undergoing major changes as old houses were demolished to make room for railway extensions. An increasing number of people were becoming slum dwellers, living on casual labour and were completely out of touch with any denomination. The area, the author wrote, 'constituted one vast mission district'.

The writer wanted it to be recognised and organised as such. Present reorganisation was 'mechanical and arbitrary'. 'Hitherto,' he wrote, 'our authorities have argued that whenever a parish arrives at a population of 10,000 or 15,000 it is ready and fit for sub-division.' Sub-division left new parishes with churches that had been built as cheaply as possible. They had no money for curates and only had the bare minimum of necessary equipment. In St Pancras, where the four ancient parishes had become thirty new ones, the problem was particularly acute.

The author called for an end to this enormously destructive process and for the implementation of a system that was better suited to the mission field that north London had become:

> Evangelisation must proceed from strong and fully equipped centres. Instead of the poor and sickly churches in out-of-the-way corners, we sorely want a few large Basilicas which will show up well in open spaces, capable of holding 2,000 with a strong staff of five or six clergy, each carefully selected, not to be a sort of jack of all trades, but for his particular vocation and ministry. Let these weak and feeble parishes with their mean, dilapidated, and ill-placed churches be boldly thrown together.[47]

It was a view that, as the twentieth century proceeded, was increasingly endorsed all over the country. In 1911 the Archbishops' Committee on Church Finance pointed out that 'each parish was a self-sufficient entity, possessing its own endowments and managing its own affairs [which lead to an] exaggerated parochialism which could not see beyond the needs and rights of the parish, and was wholly capable of changing with conditions'. Not for the last time, the 1911 report recommended that the diocese should be the essential unit of church life.

Unfortunately, and again not for the last time, the recommendations of the 1911 report were acted upon only in the most partial and reluctant of ways. The few brief decades towards the end of the nineteenth century, in which there was (nearly) one priest for every parish in the country, cast a long shadow over the following century. The fact that Anglican Church attendance only began to fall in the 1940s left the Church more optimistic and therefore much more conservative than the anonymous writer of the St Pancras pamphlet had been decades beforehand.

Reforming moves were made in the wake of the First World War, with parliament passing the Union of Benefices Measure in 1923. This enabled two parishes to be united into one benefice, but it also set an ominous precedent for the rest of the century. It may have been another half century before the Pastoral Measure of 1968 really allowed multi-parish benefices to develop and reach their potential, but the pattern of burdening incumbents with more and more duties had been set. For understandable if not justifiable reasons, the Church was determined to treat the malaise with only tentative measures and then only at the last resort. Without realising it, it had in effect started to plan for its own decline.

New Horizons in Lincolnshire

The story of the revival of the minster hypothesis starts proper in rural Lincolnshire, in the aftermath of the Second World War, with the first major experiment in team/group ministry. In 1949, the Pastoral

Reorganisation Measure gave, in the words of the then Archbishop of York, 'each diocese the power to survey its parishes as a whole and to regroup and reorganise them so that both men and money are used to the best advantage'. Nowhere was this needed more than in rural Lincolnshire where the change in agriculture and the massive decline in the number of farm workers had left many villages depopulated and many parish churches empty. In the wake of the 1949 Measure, the Diocese of Lincoln set up a Bishops' Committee of Inquiry, including both clerical and lay members, to propose changes out of which came the South Ormsby Experiment.

The South Ormsby group was made up of fifteen small parishes with twelve churches, covering an area of approximately seventy-five square miles and a population of just over 1,100. A meeting held in 1949 agreed that A.C. Smith, the existing Rector of South Ormsby (and three other parishes), would act as the rector of the whole group as parishes became vacant.

Critically, however, this was not just another example of tacking parishes together when they fell vacant and increasing the pressure on already overworked rural vicars. As Smith himself wrote about the experience in 1960, such 'temporary expedients are quite useless and, indeed, may be harmful . . . [showing] haphazard planning [and] merely staving off the day when a more permanent solution becomes imperative [by which time] it may be too late'.[48] Ultimately, the only result of such arrangements was that parishioners came to feel neglected and parsons frustrated by lack of time.

The South Ormsby Experiment was, by Smith's own admission, 'made up on the hoof'. In 1949 he became rector of four more parishes and was joined by a former schoolmaster who had been made a deacon and appointed to assist the project. The following year two more parishes became vacant and were added to the group and later in the 1950s the final parishes of Oxcombe, Ruckland, Farforth, Maidenwell and the extra-parochial chapel of ease at Worlaby also joined.

The group was not centred on one mother church as that was deemed to be overly bureaucratic and not in keeping with natural independence of villages. Instead, each church set up its own parochial administration, ran its own accounts, held its own meetings and so preserved its individuality while remaining an active member of a larger family.

The overall staff team comprised the rector, an assistant priest, a deacon, a deaconess and an honorary lay reader. Each was married and all but one had children, so staff members lived independently in three rectories that were kept on and modified for use. The staff met in parishes for matins and communion and for breakfast to discuss problems. They also held a more formal staff meeting once a week. In addition to this there were six, more social, clergy dinners per year in the various rectories, as well as the annual rural deanery conference and quiet day. The group also had an important function as a place to provide training for clergy in the work of rural ministry. Overall, a thoroughly collegiate structure was embraced in the group, with clergy working together in the same super-parish but at the same time maintaining a degree of autonomy and independence.

All but one of the staff team owned a car and so were well placed to visit parishioners in the area. Services were held around the group with the congregation moving from one church to another each Sunday, by car or by a parish bus, which was bought and run for the less mobile parishioners. A leaflet was produced to share parish news across the group.

The result was that parishioners still felt they had a clergyman living in or very near their parish and this helped maintain the sense of possession, belonging and identity that was considered very important for the area. Crucially, however, inhabitants of villages became aware of and were drawn into a wider group community.

The laity were expected to pitch in more than they had in the past. Churchwardens and sidesmen were made into an informal executive committee to be called upon when matters of policy affecting the group as a whole were considered, the idea being that they would go back to their parishes and acquaint people with the decisions that had been made on their behalf. As Smith later wrote, 'it is the laity who must provide the day-to-day efficiency for the running of the modern parish'.

Overall each parish retained its own freedom within the framework. Smith wrote, '[we were] trying to form a new community sense among the scattered parishes, most of which were far too small to sustain a flourishing, independent existence of their own'. The group was never a complete parochial unit in law but only ever an arrangement of pluralities in hands of a single rector. Today, South Ormsby does not sound particularly special, but it was a revolutionary experiment for its time and made some important conceptual leaps away from atomised parishes and towards a collegiate system that had much wider horizons than the individual parishes it had replaced.

Recognising the innovation at South Ormsby one author wrote an article in *Church and Countryside* in October 1958 suggesting that, 'the policy of plurality and union could be carried to its logical conclusion in the countryside by forming large groupings of parishes, which would be presided over by a single rector, aided by a band of assistant curates'.[49]

This 'logical conclusion' was indeed reached in a number of areas. In 1961, ten parishes in the Breckland district of Norfolk formed the Hillborough group and over the next decade seventeen groups became established in Norfolk alone. By 1970 a third of all clergy in the Norwich area were organised in this way. Each group would differ slightly in structure and nomenclature but at the same time, 'each group sought to provide for a wide area a pastoral ministry which combined on the spot pastoral care with centralised planning of services and other activities such as youth and children's work, adult education and confirmation classes'. None was centralised in quite the same way as minster churches had been, and none was founded on evangelistic principles but the collegiate, resource-pooling structure was fundamentally minster-like in its nature.

The Paul Report

It was against this background of experiment that, in January 1964, the sociologist and author, Leslie Paul, published a report entitled *The Deployment and Payment of the Clergy*. This looked at the same issues as the Diocese of Lincoln had faced in the late 1940s, but did so more broadly and in greater detail. In July 1960 the Church Assembly had passed a resolution 'that the Central Advisory Council for the Ministry be instructed to consider, in the light of changing circumstances, the system of the payment and deployment of the clergy, and to make recommendations'. Leslie Paul was asked to conduct the research.

The problems were widely recognised but he brought a new clarity to them. There were too few Anglican clergy. A national ratio of one clergyman to just over 1,000 people in 1851 had dropped slightly over the following half century to become one in 1,295 in 1901, and had then cascaded to one in 2,271 by 1951. Over the same period, the clergy had become correspondingly much older than the population average.

More worryingly, most of the clergy were in the wrong place. With the massive urbanisation of the nineteenth and twentieth centuries, what had once been 'the common-sense policy of providing one priest for every natural community' was now 'in effect . . . a haphazard distribution of men' creating a massive imbalance between the numbers of people per parish.

Paul examined the major social changes of the twentieth century – the population explosion, the increase in commuting times, the radical change in means and structure of transportation, decaying inner cities, the growth of housing estates and building of tower blocks, and the decline of village life. Each of these trends would have demanded a change in Anglican pastoral strategy, even if the Church had been well placed to deal with the situation in 1964, which it was not.

On a more intimate level Paul also looked at the increasing tendency towards smaller families and smaller, more efficient houses. He examined the prospective breakdown of community and what we would today call the problem of social capital, quoting both sociological and theological warnings for the future:

> What has been taking place, and is, indeed, still going on, is nothing less than a gigantic nation-wide social experiment, involving whole neighbourhoods and vast populations on the move and under constraint of enforced change. The happiness and even the mental health of hundreds of thousands of people depend on the way in which these large-scale migrations take place. (Dr John Barron Mays, 'New Hope in Newtown', *New Society* 47 [August 1963])

Outstanding traits of modern society are loneliness and massification. Both belong together. They imply an irrepressible drift towards virtual or actual nihilism, inner emptiness and loss of real sense of direction. (Hendrick Kraemer, *A Theology of the Laity*, 1958)[50]

The Church of England was singularly ill placed to deal with these problems. Statistics showed that the pastoral capacity in dioceses was usually in inverse proportion to density of population: the more people in an area, the fewer Anglican clergy there were.

The problems all pointed in the direction of the parish system. The Church had been too reluctant (and then too eager) in responding to the massive demographic and sociological changes of the nineteenth century. As Paul pointed out, similar changes were occurring in the post-war period. New neighbourhoods were being created through the building of housing estates and old ones demolished through slum clearance programmes. The closure of factories and pits had devastating effects on some communities and the building of motorways and flyovers had similar consequences for others. Rural areas were declining through an exodus of young people, or were being transformed by the growth of tourism, the establishment of caravan parks, changing patterns of retirement, or the increase in commuting distances. The parish structure desperately needed to reflect all of this.

Paul's analysis of the parochial deficiencies was no less acute. While recognising its historic achievement, he asked, frankly, whether it was just 'an administrative inconvenience in the deployment of men'. Church, parsonage and church hall had become plants which must be serviced and kept going at all costs, 'almost irrespective of whether people use [them] or not'. Overly fond attachment to buildings over the centuries had institutionalised the Church, leaving both the faithful laity and the general public viewing the Church as little more than the buildings it displays, 'to which the clergy are sent as of necessity'. Change was always a nightmare. 'Much evidence has come my way of the tenacity with which the laity will fight to preserve an actual church even when all pastoral justification for it has gone, and really it only encumbers the ground.' Ultimately, 'a territorial pastoral system inherited from the past and tied to its buildings must always be in trouble over the adjustment of its relatively inflexible institutions to the changing pastoral needs of a fluid society'.

The problem was even more acute in the town than in the country. The urban and suburban priests to whom Paul spoke did not think in terms of parishes at all. Parochial isolation might, on rare occasions, have helped define and foster the sense of community in rural areas, but it could never do so in towns. One priest per parish made even less sense when the parish was 'a slice cut artificially out of a tangle of urban streets and meaningless to its inhabitants' and with no more significance than the legal and administrative consequences the Church imported to it.

Collegiate ministries made even more sense in the town they did in the country. One of Paul's interviewees summarised the viewpoint popular in town and country in this way:

> [I] think that the clergy would be much more effective if they worked a lot more closely together and got to know each other better … conferences, meetings are not enough; the clergy need to meet each other more informally, perhaps more in each others' homes … [There is] real need for closer contact between parochial clergy

> who still work too much in isolation and even in compe-
> tition ... [I] cannot see any sign yet of 'group Ministry'
> becoming the norm ... but ... many of us think our work
> could be done better along such lines.

Another put it more succinctly: 'No parish should have less than two clergy. Partnerships – viz. doctors – prove best.'

The conclusion was as clear as it was unpalatable: 'The inflexibility of the existing parochial system is an impediment to the exercise of the Church's pastoral ministry, but equally productive of despair among the clergy.'

Paul's solution was to work with the preference for and trend towards group ministries in such a way as would be a step closer to the minster church model: 'What is needed is a new parochial form to permit group or team ministries formed of clergy on an equal basis to come into existence.' This would involve uniting benefices, so that one freehold would be created, which would then be held and enjoyed by a corporate body, such as 'a college of clergy of which all members ... would have equal rights and of which the chief or head or leader would properly be called a dean: perhaps "town dean" to distinguish him from rural dean'. In such a parish, all clergy would have the status of vicars or incumbents and would be subject to the same 'lease-hold' or terminable tenure as incumbents generally.

Rather than being a wholly innovative concept, this arrangement would, as Paul recognised 'resemble in some measure cathedral chapters or colleges'. This plan was one step on from the South Ormsby experiment. Individual, autonomous parishes still remained but there now emerged collegiate churches which, although not superior in any 'mother church' sense, were certainly larger and wider ranging:

The parochial area of such a college ought sensibly to be called, because of its size and importance, a 'major parish'. Thus without the destruction of the parochial system, there would come into existence major parishes run by colleges of clergy side by side with minor ones run by individual incumbents.

And with a nod towards early Christian pastoral organisation, Paul wrote: 'A truly corporate ministry would thus come legally alive for the first time in the parishes since early monastic days.'

Importantly, a fundamental part of this overall plan was the participation of the laity. Paul advocated a lay pastoral system, with weekday house communions in each street, pastoral aid to lay professionals and new constitutional forms of independent lay cooperation, such as lay deanery councils. Provision would be made for full-time lay workers to be members of the college and every proposal for major parishes or new rural deanery forms would be invalid unless it provided for lay training and lay responsibilities, such as lay street groups, house churches and independent lay initiatives:

> If generally the narrow parochial system is to give way to ministries which corporately serve a borough, a rural district, a new town or some meaningful social and parochial unit, it will be imperative to carry organisation as deeply as possible into the life of the neighbourhood, so that the Church becomes the Church in the street and in the homes, and not just an appendage to the vicarage.

Paul's proposal was minster-like in a considerable number of ways. It was resolutely collegiate, it placed much emphasis on the local presence and on the importance of the laity, and it was determined to develop the training capacities of churches. It was not minster-like in every way, by any means, but it was a decisive step forwards from South Ormsby.

Paul recognised that total transformation of the parochial system was neither immediately feasible nor practicable. The old had to be allowed to live with the new and encouraged to grow alongside it. His plan was to introduce new forms of ministry into areas, such as isolated rural areas, decaying inner suburbs and rapidly developing fringes of expanding conurbations, where the old parochial system had broken down. Whatever happened, the approach was to be gradual and organic, rather than sudden and artificial:

> One begins with an informal group ministry and out of joint pastoral efforts, area acts of worship, new forms of lay consultation, one develops an official ... form of joint service: out of such a loose federation it would be possible to proceed, at the right moment, to the establishment of a major parish.

Paul was aware of the challenges of even such a gradual and gentle approach. But he was even more aware of the alternative: 'Though the difficulties stare us in the face, the alternatives are chilling – to do nothing, which means to abandon the nation to its religious decline and the clergy to their isolation.'

Sadly, the response to his proposal was less balanced and clear sighted. While radicals saw in it the dawn of a genuine new hope, others were horror struck. Many churchmen accused Paul of adopting a sociological and therefore superficial approach to the Church of England that displayed a lack of spiritual understanding and regarded the ordained ministry as a professional career instead of a divine vocation. Paul should not assume that the clergy were branch managers of a chain store. The responsibilities and duties of a clergyman in a particular parish could not be assessed on statistics alone.

Criticism focused on four areas. First, there was patronage. The priesthood was a vocation. A priest was not called to be 'a pawn on a vast, impersonal, bureaucratic chessboard', as the *Church Times* described it. Secondly, modifying the freehold would deprive a priest of his independence. Thirdly, centralisation would import a civil service mentality, and fourthly, reforms would deflect energy from more important mission and pastoral care. As Canon Paul Welsby has written:

> A sad thread running through so much of the criticism was the implication that somehow it was less than godly to be businesslike and efficient and that Christian stewardship might be applicable to financial matters but not to the organisation of the Church's ministry.[51]

Among the more positive responses, *The Church of England Newspaper* wrote that, 'some such policy as that advocated by the Report must be adopted if the Church is to survive and be effective in the 1970s and 1980s'.[52] In fact, reforms were not implemented after the Report's publication and it was only twenty years later, and then in a modified form, that Paul's recommendations were seriously adopted.

Faith in . . . more Reports

Leslie Paul's recommendations may not have been immediately adopted but ensuing years did see the parish structure increasingly modified. The 1968 Pastoral Measure provided a legal basis for further group and team developments, so that within fifteen years there were ninety-one group ministries and 333 team ministries. The following year, in an increasingly ecumenical atmosphere, the Sharing of Church Buildings Measure allowed other denominations to use Anglican churches and made it lawful to build new churches on a shared basis with certain limitations and conditions. Local Ecumenical Partnerships were set up, in which the parish structure took second place to the details of inter-denominational cooperation. Inevitably, most new areas of ecumenical cooperation were in new housing estates that lacked the weight of traditional structures to obstruct new initiatives, but in some areas well-established denominational boundaries were broken down in favour of ecumenical ones. By the end of the 1970s there were over 300 LEPs, most of which shared buildings.

The problems analysed within the Paul report did not, however, go away. In the mid-1970s the Church again looked at how to address the imbalance between urban and rural areas and this time came up with a way of weighting four key factors, population, places of worship, size of area and electoral role, in order to dictate strategy for clergy deployment. This was the logistical and businesslike approach for which many had criticised Leslie Paul but it was still, in effect, a band-aid. It succeeded in redeploying clergy along more practical lines, but it also resulted in the rapid and widespread development of multi-parish benefices and failed to address the equally pressing problems of dwindling congregations and resources, proportionally more costly restoration bills, and ever more stressed and isolated clergy. It was not until the Tiller Report was published, nearly two decades after Leslie Paul's work, that these problems were examined in detail again.

The Tiller Report began with a depressingly familiar analysis of the problems. The existing parish structure may have been omnipresent, readily available, local and very public but its weaknesses now far outweighed its strengths. Its boundaries were meaningless. It isolated ministers. It demanded maintenance rather than mission. It was 'liable to become a refuge for those who appear in the community as lovers of traditionalism for its own sake'.[53] It limited links to other church agencies and was ill-equipped to deal with the ever fragmenting, atomised, ill-connected, transient communities which lived within but worked and socialised outside parish boundaries. And on top of all this, it was unsustainable. John Tiller wrote, 'The actual number of clergy available for parish work is now about 1,000 less than the minimum required.'[54]

It was not all bad news. The diocese had increased in significance as the basic unit for the deployment of clergy. There was more ecumenical and trans-parochial cooperation. Opportunities for specialist ministry had increased. The vitality of the laity was more in evidence now than ever before.

Nevertheless, even if the Paul report had helped move the Church towards a more effective and efficient use of existing pastoral structures, it was still really just a case of stretching resources further. As one writer put it, 'The Church, because of its dynamic conservatism, [has] become satisfied with presiding over its own elaborate and time-consuming funeral service.'[55]

Controversially, Tiller suggested that 'there comes a point at which the maintenance of a full-time nation-wide pastoral ministry available to all through the traditional parochial system proves incapable of being sustained'. Tiller, like Paul, recognised the importance of local ministry. The Church could not and should not pull

out of 'uneconomic' communities. It was not a bank or a
retailer and should not behave like one. It had a responsibility in a way commercial organisations did not. But,
crucially, that responsibility was to its parishioners and
not to its historic buildings or traditional community
role. The task was to maintain presence without being
tortured on the rack of a painfully anachronistic
parochial structure.

Tiller's answer was to use a quasi-minster approach,
much of which chimed with Paul's recommendations.
According to him the local church was to work on three
levels. At the most intimate were cell or house groups,
which would meet regularly, pastor one another and
become involved with local community projects.

Above these was the 'public congregation' that operated in the parish or local geographical area as already
existed. The difference between these and the existing
parish churches was that these would be in the care not
of a parish priest but of a leadership team of local ministers and others working on a diocesan basis. They
would regularly convene and serve as witness of the
Church in the locality: 'The local church will decide
what forms of ministry are appropriate in its own situation for prayer, teaching, evangelism and pastoral care.'
Finally, at the level above the 'public congregation' there
was the deanery, which would become the area of local
church government and function like a group ministry.[56]

The strategy stopped short of appointing minster
churches within minster parishes but many minster
principles lay behind the plan. Christian communities
would become self-operative, in a way that pre- and
early parochial Anglo-Saxon villages were. Each 'should
accept their vocation to be the Church and become
responsible for their own ministry'. Ordained ministers
were to have a pastoral function but this was secondary

to the mutual pastoring of the laity and, crucially, to the pressing need for mission. 'The stipendiary ministers of the Church should be placed according to the priorities of mission.'

This missionary function would also be pressed upon the diocese. 'Bishops will lead a "task force" of priests and deacons, some stipendiary, others in secular employment, who will foster the Church's mission and provide resources which are lacking in local churches.' Deaneries and, above them, dioceses would function as resource centres for local churches in need of help. Moreover, this resourcing was to maintain a fluidity that was central to the minster idea. 'Many diocese priests and deacons will have to be seconded to local churches which are not strong enough to provide their own ministry but will not become ensnared in a benefice.'

Tiller's recommendations were challenging and like Paul's accepted only partially, by stealth and through necessity rather than choice. Tiller had written passionately that 'it is verging on blasphemy to spend hundreds of thousands of pounds restoring an under-used church in the midst of urban deprivation'. His words had an eerie prescience given the recommendations of the controversial *Faith in the City* report, commissioned around the time his report was made public and published two years later.

This was not primarily concerned with pastoral reorganisation, being commissioned instead to 'examine the strengths, insights, problems and needs of the Church's life and mission in Urban Priority Areas'. Nevertheless, it inevitably touched on parochial issues as part of its remit and, once again, arrived at principles which were minster-based in all but name.

The Tiller Report advised that the traditional parochial system 'although necessary for maintaining an Anglican presence in Urban Priority Areas has its limitations, and is in need of reform'. An Urban Priority Area church, according to *Faith in the City*, had to take its neighbourhoods seriously but as neighbourhoods 'defined by people living in them – where they begin and end, significant meeting places, amenities, etc.' rather than as arcane or theoretical ecclesiastical boundaries. Ecclesiastical units should be based on where people were rather than the legal niceties of the existing parish structure. The report concluded that parochial boundaries should be revised 'to relate more closely to such neighbourhoods,' that 'small neighbourhood-based worship centres' needed to be developed, and 'that partnership in ministry is essential to the development of an effective Church in Urban Priority Areas'.

The *Faith in the City* parochial recommendations were swamped under Conservative criticism that the report's passionate concern for the poor and marginalised was Marxist. In fairness, it was never especially concerned with parochial re-evaluation, unlike the Bishop of Chelmsford's Commission on Diocesan Strategy, which was published three years later. This finally found the words that so many other reports had been searching for. It suggested 'the possibility of establishing a minster church tradition rather than a parish church tradition and so building on church centres already noted for their strength and possibly making them the focal centres of rural deaneries'. At long last, after a thousand or so years of silence, if not complete absence, the minster returned to England.

The idea was again brought up in *Faith in the City*'s less controversial successor *Faith in the Countryside*, which was published in 1990. This revealed that some dioceses had come up with the solution of basing team ministries on market towns and that during the report's consultation period the Bishop of Sherborne gave evidence which supported the idea of 'following a minster pattern in which clergy would live in or close to a focal market town and would minister to the town and its hinterland'. 'The need for a focal person in each parish,' the report went on, 'would be provided by a locally ordained diaconate.'

The *Faith in the Countryside* report had mixed feelings about this approach. On the one hand, given the Church's dwindling resources it was a sensible, perhaps mandatory solution. Less cynically, it answered the real need to end clergy isolation and give mutual support to clergymen and soon clergywomen. Nevertheless, there was an understandable recognition that the scheme 'would mean the further withdrawal of stipendiary clergy from residence in genuinely rural areas', making rural parishes feel still more marginalised. Minster churches might, if not evolved and structured properly, herald as many problems as they would solutions.

Historical Reasons – A Brief Conclusion

It could be possible to double the length of this chapter with other examples of how history appears to be moving inexorably towards (or back to) a minster church system. A 1993 paper on rethinking pastoral strategy entitled *The Future of Our Past* suggested that while there should not be wholesale abandonment of the parochial system there was need to develop 'major benefices' centred on a minster-like system.

More recently, several reports of the Scottish Church Initiative for Union have examined in detail the prospects of a maxi-parish, 'a designated area, recognised by the local people as a definable community [which] generally speaking . . . would be the area of a sizeable town and those surrounding areas which focus in on it'.[57]

This area would incorporate up to seven worship centres, thus allowing the continuation of different worship traditions. A ministry team of full- and part-time staff, elected from local church councils, would administer it. And it would employ specialist lay people who were now beyond the reach of most parish congregations. Time and again the same themes emerge.

At the end of her history of the English parish, Anthea Jones wrote, 'The history of the parish shows [how much] variety, experiment and change there has been within and between communities and townships.'[58] History shows that these experiments have come in fits and starts. The twenty-first century looks like it is going to be one of these periods, although for reasons of necessity rather than choice. After a handful of prescient but unheeded calls in the early twentieth century, the South Ormsby Experiment, the Paul Report, the Tiller Report, the Bishop of Chelmsford's Commission on Diocesan Strategy and the *Faith in the Countryside* report, among many others have all been slowly groping their way towards a new pastoral structure for England. The path along which they have been wandering has in fact been one that leads us back 1,300 years to the Anglo-Saxon minster church.

To add a personal perspective to this story of the seemingly inexorable direction of history, had I known about Paul, Tiller and the others when I first wrote about the minster churches four years ago, I think I would have given up there and then. The temptation to think, 'What's the point? People – people with rather more influence than me – have been here and done that long ago', would have been almost overwhelming. 'If Leslie Paul can be ignored, then Nick Spencer is sure to be!'

Yet, coming across these examples and plans over the last year or so has been anything but dispiriting. Indeed, rather than being daunted by prior excursions into this area, every minster or quasi-minster proposal I have encountered has persuaded me that I am on the right track and that the idea is not simply a straw in the wind.

Perhaps more importantly, every proposal I have read has convinced me that this is going to happen anyway *whether we like it or not*. The English parish structure is unsustainable. God is pruning his church (or, more precisely, this small corner of it) perhaps in order to make it more fruitful.

The trends, be they social, ecclesiastical or historical, all point in one direction. The question the Established Church faces is quite simple: will it allow these conditions to dictate its strategy or will it, to use a word popular in modern management-speak, be 'proactive' in its preparations and try to shape circumstances rather than be shaped by them? And if it is intent on shaping its future, as I believe it must, precisely how does it plan to go about it?

It is to this final question that we now turn.

Further Reading

Faith in the City: The Report of the Archbishop of Canterbury's Commission on Urban Priority Areas (Church House Publishing, 1985)

Faith in the Countryside: The Report of the Archbishop's Commission on Rural Areas (Churchman Publishing, 1990)

Leslie Paul, *The Deployment and Payment of the Clergy* (Church Information Office, 1964)

A.C. Smith, *The South Ormsby Experiment* (London: SPCK, 1960)

John Tiller, *A Strategy for the Church's Ministry* (London: CIO Publishing, 1983)

7

Going Back For the Future

One of the oldest and most unfair slurs on the teaching profession is the saying that 'those who can't do, teach'. It would be far more reasonable to say, 'those who can't do, write'.

Writing a book on the future of the English parish and looking towards a time in which it is based on the Anglo-Saxon minster model has many challenges but even more advantages. In a book you can focus on all the fantastic benefits of your idea and quietly sweep the difficulties under the carpet. In a book you have an undisturbed platform on which you can parade your thoughts without fear of interruption, criticism or abuse. In a book you tend not to have to deal with people's lethargy, conservatism, over-enthusiasm, miscomprehension, or plain antagonism. In a book you have the privilege of releasing your ideas and then standing back to watch other people try to round them up and actually make something concrete of them. It is not always easy to write, but it is easier than doing.

For this reason, it seems only reasonable that I should conclude with some suggestions on how the

Anglo-Saxon minster system might actually be implemented in twenty-first century England. It is one thing to claim that the minster system is better suited to modern England than the medieval parish system, and then to show that there are convincing social, ecclesiastical and historical reasons why this is so. It is quite another *making* it so.

Inevitably, the suggestions that follow are tentative and may be easily criticised. I have avoided giving specific named examples, not because they do not exist – a number of churches, such as St Thomas' Crookes; Sunderland Minster; St Paul's Howell Hill; St James' Gerrard's Cross, and Holy Trinity Brompton, to name but a few, are minster churches in all but name (and *in* name in the case of Sunderland!) – but because I do not want to give the impression that the future is simply a matter of imitating churches that are 'already there'. As will become clear, local variety and innovation is critical to the whole idea.

What follows, therefore, is not intended to be a prescriptive programme for the Church of England in the twenty-first century but more a series of suggestions to provoke response and maybe even action.

Getting started

Before even beginning to implement a minster model in England, some ground rules for the process need to be outlined. These should govern the way the process is conducted and perhaps act as overarching principles for the Anglican Church in the twenty-first century. Overall, the transformation needs to be flexible, organic, gradual and persevering.

Flexible

One of the fundamental, defining characteristics of the Anglo-Saxon minster system was its local flexibility. As a decentralised, independent and largely ad hoc system it was both locally owned and capable of adapting to the particularities of its environment.

In a country which today ranges from inner city Manchester, through leafy Surbiton, to semi-rural Kent, and then to wholly rural Cumbria, this is a particularly important principle to adhere to. One of the basic reasons why we need a minster approach today is because a one size, one vicar per one parish approach is no longer appropriate, let alone viable. It would be quite wrong to fall into the same error with the minster system.

What this in effect means is that localities must be encouraged to *own* and *define* their minster parish in a way that allows them to tailor it to their particularities. It is neither right nor feasible to legislate the size, population or number of churches within a minster parish. Only local knowledge and concern can do that.

Organic

Closely linked to the idea of flexibility is the recognition that the approach must be organic. In other words, this is not a strategy for the bishops to implement; rather it is for clergy and congregations to initiate and shape. Change has to come from within parishes rather than upon them.

What this in effect means is that the idea has to be sold to Anglican Christians up and down the country. They must start to think of themselves less as parishioners of their local church and more as 'parishioners' of their local minster.

There is an obvious catch-22 here. How can people think in a minster parish fashion in order to fashion a minster parish? You can only see yourself as part of a minster if one already exists.

This is, of course, true, but it is not an insuperable barrier. What it, in essence, means is that congregations should become aware, for example, of the reality of the local deanery instead of just the parish. In one sense, this will be easy, given the proportion of church-goers who cross parish boundaries to worship, but in another it will be tough, feeling, at least at first, rather unnatural.

A minster sense could be fostered by revolving preachers around local churches regularly, joint PCC meetings, shared worship sessions, shared children's work or OAP luncheon clubs, or any other number of possible contact points. Each of these should precede any *official* abolition of parish boundaries and integration of church responsibilities.

Gradual

It is not enough for the approach to be organic; it will also need to be gradual. This should be obvious but our eagerness to see change can often blind us to it.

We should never forget that we are effectively looking at changing the oldest public structure in England and even though we should not credit the myth that things have not altered in a millennium, we should disabuse ourselves of the notion that the process will be quick.

Realistically speaking this is a transition that should not take less than a generation to make and may well take two or three.

Persevering

Taking time will take courage. The one thing that can be guaranteed of the whole process is that it will be criticised. People will carp about surrender, the white flag being waved, an admission of failure, the death of Christian Britain, etc.

Inevitably much resistance will be down to plain, old-fashioned conservatism: new means worse. In such instances, a clear case must be made for the long-term unsustainability of the status quo. As already observed, if we do not end up sacrificing the wrong things, we will end up sacrificing the right ones.

In other cases, criticism will be more realistic and better thought out, and in these instances local flexibility and autonomy must come into play. Where there are genuine objections they need to be taken on board and used to modify the system, rather than simply ignored.

Above all, we need always to bear in mind that parochial reorganisation should be an exercise of regrouping rather than retreat. Rather than recoiling back into its shell, the Church needs to see the transition as one of putting its house in order so that it may reach out more fruitfully in the twenty-first century.

The Minster Church

With these guidelines in place we can consider what a minster system might be like by looking first at the minster church itself.

The minster parish

Once the mindset of parishioners has been expanded so that they feel some sense of affinity with those

Christians in the locality, rather than just those who attend the same building on a Sunday, a precise minster area would be defined. These will vary hugely and should be determined at least as much by local clergy and congregations as by episcopal edict.

Factors that would influence the decision will include local population density, number of churches and congregations, size of electoral roles, existing parish sizes and financial circumstances. They might also include local communication networks, shopping centres, leisure facilities and schools. The unit will, as far as possible, need to be a 'natural' creation, although in many areas this will be almost impossible. Local council administrative districts or constituency wards may help, as might geographic features (the criterion that Anglo-Saxon minster builders would have appreciated).

There is much merit in surveying parishioners. Without too much effort, it would be possible to have a selection from various congregations record a brief geography/time diary, which would detail where and when they travel and for what purposes. Such an approach would foster the sense of inclusion and involvement among parishioners and have the advantage of producing minster parishes which were, as far as any local geographical boundaries are today, genuinely relevant.

First among equals

While the boundaries are being considered, it will be important to ascertain and recognise the minster church(es) in the area, a consideration which will itself powerfully influence the choice of the boundaries in the first place. This is likely to be one of the most challenging tasks as people will almost certainly perceive the minster church to be the 'superior' one, in the way that mother churches were 'superior' when the original minster system broke up.

It cannot be stressed enough that this is not so. Minster churches would certainly be the central and 'main' church in any minster parish. However, they would not be superior in the sense of having direct or absolute authority over other churches in the minster parish. This would be for a number of reasons. First, *all* parishioners in the minster parish would 'belong' to the minster church and have a say in how it is run. Secondly, most would attend the minster church at some point in an average month. Thirdly, all vicars within the minster parish would be officially incumbent at the minster, and all curates, non-stipendiary ministers, and lay members would be 'based' there. Fourthly, the minster's fundamental role within the minster parish would be as *a resource centre*, providing whatever the other local churches are not able to. In this way, the minster church would not simply be the biggest or 'most successful' parish church in the area, elevated to a position of authority as a reward for its success; rather, it would be the 'area church', to whom everybody belonged, which everyone helped run and from which everyone could draw support.

These factors should foster a broad-based sense of corporate ownership and would help make the minster church 'first among equals' rather than the 'supreme' or 'best' church. It should ideally play almost as much of a role in parishioners' lives as their 'old' parish church did.

The choice of the minster church would, of course, depend on local circumstances, but would inevitably include considerations, such as locality, position, history, building size, versatility, fabric condition, finances, and congregation size and nature.

It should not be impossible for any minster parish to contain more than one minster church, although this would complicate legal matters. Such an arrangement would, again, depend on local circumstances, but if the total congregation for an obvious minster area was too large for one minster church, or if, conversely, no one church was an obvious minster candidate but two were equally well equipped and positioned, rather than separate two smaller minster parishes, it might be advisable to maintain two minster churches in one minster parish. Both minster churches would provide distinct services but would still meet and discuss local strategy together as and when they needed to.

Whether the minster church would be an existing or wholly new edifice would also be a matter for local deliberation. There are obvious advantages in new buildings, in that they can be used and modified in ways which existing ones cannot. Moreover, expensive as new church buildings obviously are, the on-going restoration and renovation costs of an historic building may, in the end, prove false economy.

This does not mean that existing church buildings are expendable or irrelevant – they quite clearly are not, either for their congregations, who are often mightily attached to them, or non-attending parishioners who are often equally favourably disposed. It is, instead, to insist that the Church is made of people not stone, and that if it comes to a straight choice between the two, as undoubtedly it will in certain circumstances, we must always go with the former.

In reality, this will be far more of an issue with 'local' churches than minster ones (and will be dealt with accordingly below), but it *may* mean that in any one minster parish it will be logistically necessary and financially sensible (in the long run) to sell three, vast, unheatable, unattractive, inadequate, Victorian, barn-like edifices and erect in their place one state-of-the-art, modern, adaptable building.

Whatever the precise arrangements are, financially the minster will be one unit, a fact that will undoubtedly encourage the drive for unity. Vicars, curates and other staff members will be employed and 'paid' by the minster, which will also be responsible for the diocesan payments and, crucially, any financial decisions to be made concerning the upkeep and renovation of ecclesiastical buildings within the minster parish.

This financial arrangement will invariably result in some tension, particularly when the minster unit still feels artificial. But, in reality, what financial arrangements do not breed tension? The trite but true observation that 'whoever pays the piper calls the tune' suggests that monetary unity will be essential if the minster parish is to work.

The minster staff

The minster church would be a collegiate church. It would be the official base for all ordained clergy in the minster parish and they would be joint incumbents of that minster church, rather than separate incumbents of existing local parish churches.

This is important. The sense of isolation and individualised ownership currently fostered by the parish system needs to be countered. Minster clergy would consciously be required to pull together for the good of the area, rather than the good of the local parish.

There would almost certainly need to be a head pastor of a minster who would have final authority over and responsibility for the business of the minster, but this is, in effect, no different from the current role of team rector.

Regular corporate worship, prayer and strategy meetings would encourage a sense of collegiate identity. Clergy may or may not live near the minster church, depending on local circumstances, although a truly collegiate, dormitory arrangement is not envisaged.

Instead, local clergy would have special responsibility for particular local churches. They would be the first point of contact for members of that congregation, be accountable to the minster for the congregation and represent it on the central minster 'council', alongside members of its PCC.

Such an arrangement would, of course, present real challenges. The *Faith in the City* report mentioned how 'the problems of teams and groups may have [in the past] deterred some from collaborative ministry', and there can be no disguising the fact that collegiate ministry does not come naturally to everyone. It is not prioritised in training colleges, not encouraged by the parish system and not helped by the intricate doctrinal backbiting that Christians sometimes specialise in. Nevertheless, these are obstacles than can and, indeed, must be overcome.

A collegiate minster system would counter the loneliness, sense of isolation, and sometimes dangerous autonomy of members of the clergy. Perhaps more importantly, it would allow them to specialise. Although minster clergy would have responsibility for 'local' churches, they would also be recognised for their particular abilities throughout the minster parish. Those with a special talent for teaching, youth work, worship, social action, evangelism, conducting baptisms, weddings and funerals, pastoral work, etc. would, as far as possible, become the first port-of-call for those minster parishioners requiring that service. This would not mean that they would never do those things that they would otherwise have been doing week in week out at their old parish church and indeed, in their role as minster-vicar for 'local' congregations, they may still be required to perform such roles. Nevertheless, the collegiate minster system should enable a more efficient and productive distribution of resources across the locality and counter any needless duplication.

The other way in which the minster church would be collegiate is in its inclusion of non-ordained members on the staff. Minster churches would act as training grounds for those considering ordination, but also offer the opportunity for part-time ministry for those Christians who wished to share their working lives between their church and elsewhere. The all-or-nothing nature of the vast majority of 'official' ministry in England is understandable but regrettable. The collegiate role of a minster church would enable non-ordained members of the congregation to participate more fully in church life and strategy, and to experience valuable, coalface training for those who are considering ordination.

The minster congregation

As already observed, a sense of the minster parish should already have been instilled in the local congregations. A fully established minster system will effectively require a dual role and identity from parishioners. The first will be their role vis-à-vis their 'local' church, which will be discussed below. The second will be their role as minster members. They would all be members of their local minster church, even if they do not worship there every Sunday. They would be on the minster directory, asked to contribute to the minster services, encouraged to attend the appropriate Sunday services and able to enjoy the pastoral and other services provided by the minster parish, as indeed would non-church attending parishioners of the minster parish.

The minster services

The minster church would really come into its own in its provision of services. The combination of shrinking congregations, constant church numbers and crippling fabric costs means that today many congregations are unable to provide the services they want to or to reach out to the local community in the way they want to. The pooling of resources integral to a minster church would counter this problem.

The obvious services that a minster would provide are those that already exist in many churches but done more efficiently, professionally and fruitfully. Meetings would include youth services, where a critical mass is all-important, mothers and toddlers groups, homeless outreach projects and mentoring systems.

The minster's real strength, however, would come in its provision of services quite outside those of the parish church. An example of this might be the local business centre. In much the same way as Anglo-Saxon minsters acted as local business centres, minster churches could provide bases freelance and remote workers who prefer not to be confined to their homes. Rooms could be available for mini-offices, hot-desking, broadband connection and meetings. Alternatively, space could be rented to any of the huge number of small Christian charities and businesses that operate across the country, or, indeed, any other small business whose interests and methods are in accordance with the minster's Christian principles. Obviously, such an arrangement would work on a commercial basis, as it would in any other situation, and would also demand a relatively new minster building, but there is no reason why minster churches should not take advantage of trends in teleworking to offer this modern service.

Another example would be in capitalising on the modern political emphasis on localism. For various reasons, all political parties currently have a heavy inclination towards local autonomy. Tony Blair typified this in a speech he made in 2002:

> After five years in government I know only too well that passing legislation, or making a speech will not solve vandalism on estates, raise standards in secondary schools, look after the elderly at risk. The job of government is to provide investment, support and infrastructure for those trying to solve problems at the local level.

The government's real problem is that there are not as many local bodies willing or able to assume this responsibility as they would like, and this is one role a minster church could fulfil. This is not to suggest that minster churches become local government offices but rather to indicate that, in the same way as church schools provide one of the most effective sources of education in the country, a well equipped, collegiate minster church might play an active, government-supported role in solving social problems at a local level.

Some will complain that this would take the Church too far from its core role of communicating the gospel and while a sense of caution is necessary, such a view tends to fall into the sacred-secular divide. There are no areas of society in which God is not interested and there are many ways of communicating the gospel other than from the pulpit.

A third opportunity lies in minster churches providing theological education. As already noted, the collegiate element of the minster church would mix ordained and lay members and it could do so in such a way as to provide part of the official training for curates. If the minster system is to be established, there would be a real need to teach ordinands how to work closely alongside other ministers. While theological colleges would be able to do that to some degree, minster churches would provide a more practical and complete opportunity for such training.

In a similar, if less official way, minsters might provide the opportunity for teenagers to spend a paid 'gap' year between school and university, offering them the education and experience which their current 'local' church cannot.

Another possibility would be for minsters to offer art and drama opportunities to interested parties. Although this is already offered by a number of churches, one way of fostering minster-parish identity would be to write and stage plays using the talents of parishioners across the parish. Such a project might even see the return of mystery plays to town centres and village greens on public holidays following the tradition of the guilds over 500 years ago.

Whatever else the minster offers, it is imperative that it has an active network/directory, preferably one that is on-line. In one respect, this is not a new idea at all. *Faith in the Countryside* mentioned, over ten years ago, 'that some deaneries have produced directories of members who will help or advise on certain subjects'. It continued, 'they have enabled parishes to share their problems and they have supported deanery projects ranging from local youth work to overseas community development'.

This is precisely the way in which the minster network should work, operating firmly on the principle that church family members are there to help one another whenever possible, rather than occasionally on a Sunday. The more the entire minster congregation uses and contributes to the minster network, and the better developed the minster website is, the more effective the church will be within the community.

These are just a handful of examples of how a minster church might be able to offer unique and useful services to its congregation and to the wider community. Some churches are already offering these, boasting conference centres, day nurseries, after-school clubs, sports and fitness suites, health centres, National Vocational Qualification training colleges, and even beauty parlours. Exactly which services a minster could and should provide would depend, once again, on local circumstances and cannot be centrally prescribed, but it should be clear that the opportunity is there to play a role which our fragmented communities are crying out for and which the Church, currently saddled with its outdated structure, is unable to provide.

The 'Local' Church

The Anglo-Saxon minster system was distinctly two-tiered, with minster clergy travelling to and teaching and pastoring local communities that were without clergy or churches of their own. This was an integral part of the model and did as much as anything else to spread Christianity across England long after England was, by name at least, Christian.

It is also an integral part of the modern minster model, countering any tendencies the plan might otherwise have towards retreat, economisation or centralisation. Having minster churches is not a substitute for having 'local' churches nor, to repeat myself, is it a cloak for an ecclesiastical branch closure programme.

The 'local' congregation

What the minster system *does* require is a redefinition of the role and the purpose of the 'local' church. As they stand, parish churches *are* the Anglican Church in England. Cathedral chapters and the variety of army, hospital and school chaplains are relatively small appendages to the body of the Church which exists in the bricks, mortar, hearts and lives of the local parish.

In the minster model, the 'local' congregation would still exist but *as the local presence of the minster congregation*. The minster network would be the body of the Church across the country and *all* church members would be affiliated to their local minster church. The minster team, in conference with 'local' congregations would then decide what role the 'local' congregation should play.

As already observed, there is good evidence to suggest that whatever the size of a church it needs to act small. Smaller gatherings give each individual greater weight, help people feel wanted and prevent absentees slipping through the net. This is exactly the role to be played by the 'local' church. Whereas the minster can offer the services and the worship that the local church cannot, the local congregation offers the intimacy, friendship and support that the minster congregation cannot.

The means by which this approach might develop will vary. One model would be for all church members to attend their local minster church on Sundays and participate in its communal life and to meet during the week at their 'local' church, in much the same way as cell and house groups do, providing that the local church has been adapted to this function.

Alternatively, 'local' congregations could continue meeting in the local church on Sundays, as at present, but attend the minster church one Sunday a month, to participate in broader minster-parish business and worship. Such an arrangement could also take place alongside weekday house or cell group meetings.

A third option would be for the local congregation to attend the minster church three Sundays a month. The minster congregation, or a sizeable proportion of it, would then join the local congregation on the fourth Sunday and fill out the local church, making it a special celebration to which local, non-Christian parishioners might be invited.

Whatever the precise arrangements, 'local' congregations would be far smaller than the minster one and would be made up of small ('house', 'cell') groups itself, in such a way to ensure that everyone counts. In addition, whatever the size and attendance pattern of the 'local' congregation, members would be able and encouraged to use and contribute to the services provided by the local minster, particularly those outside the 'normal' business of the Church. In an age of ubiquitous communication technology and easy transport, a minster community, although needing to be rooted and gathered in some physical way, should be able to flourish, whatever the particular local circumstances.

The 'local' church for the local congregation

The single biggest barrier to the implementation of the minster system is the existence of a vast network of architecturally priceless, ancient, often listed churches and the wrath and indignation which any questioning of their existence provokes. This is the stone on which the whole idea threatens to be broken to pieces.

At the risk of repeating myself, I emphasise again that the minster idea does not entail bulldozing or mothballing these buildings. What it does is insist that they are assessed frankly and honestly.

This assessment involves three basic questions. What are these buildings? What are they for? Who are they for? Too often we give the answers: 'churches', 'worship' and 'Christians', when in fact the real answers are 'museums', 'visiting' and 'tourists'. This is at the core of the issue.

The modern world, perhaps because it has such short time horizons itself and is so powerfully driven by short-term motives, is obsessed with the idea of preserving the old and antiquated. And no one who has stood alone in a silent, medieval country church at dusk in summertime can fail to see the validity of this desire.

The point at which it becomes invalid, however, is when we insist that these buildings have to be preserved and restored in such a way as to maintain their historic glories *and* that they can be used by a living, breathing, worshipping congregation. They cannot. You cannot do both and to think otherwise is simply to short-change one party, usually the congregation.

The honest answer to those questions, which in a minster system would be asked by the minster college and the relevant local congregation, should dictate what role these buildings have in the future. Some small, ancient, architecturally exquisite parish churches will indeed have lively, warm, active, friendly, supportive congregations, who animate local life and remain an integral part of the locality. In these instances, there is every reason for the minster parish to maintain the local church for the local congregation, even if that local congregation meets there only twice a month because it is participating in minster worship on the other Sundays.

At the other end of the scale, some parish churches will, despite being ancient and architecturally exquisite, be empty virtually all year round, without any amenities whatsoever, largely ignored by the local community (if one still exists) and, if one is being honest, with no future as a home for a worshipping congregation. In such instances, a serious renegotiation is demanded. Whether that is with English Heritage, the Churches Conservation Trust or some other body that wishes to assume the rights over and responsibilities for the building will, again, depend on local circumstances. The bottom line, however, is that if the nation wants to maintain a string of ecclesiastical *heritage centres* across the country, it needs to be prepared to pay for them.

More likely than either of these two options is some third way between them, i.e. a small, local parish church which is used regularly by a small congregation and infrequently by a wider circle for fêtes, marriages, Christingle services and the like, but is still deeply cherished and loved by the local community who would be horrified were anything to happen to it and are prepared to fight tooth-and-nail to prevent any changes.

These buildings also demand a renegotiation. In these instances, there seems to be much merit in some form of shared ownership. The congregation, again affiliated to the local minster church, might be responsible for and meet in the chancel when they choose, while at the same time leaving the nave to be used and maintained by the local community. This, in effect, would be hardly different to the medieval arrangement whereby the priest had responsibility for the chancel and the congregation for the nave.

The idea may at first sound impractical, and it is true that medieval disputes of responsibility between priests and congregations were legion, but there is no reason why it should not be workable. Various parish churches in England have recently been used for local shops, cash points, community centres, crèches and even police stations. There is no reason why this should not be extended to include cybercafes, night shelters or OAP day centres.

Of course, such uses will demand modifications but that is a price worth paying if a local community wishes to keep its most important building at the heart of the community. If, alternatively, the community wishes to keep their church – chancel and nave – as a museum piece, that should also be permissible *if they are prepared to take practical and financial responsibility for it.* What is not acceptable under a minster model is pretending a local church is a living, breathing, worshipping entity while treating it like a museum.

Of course, not all parish churches are listed (much as it might seem that way sometimes). For those that are not the same three-way discussion – between minster college, local congregation and local community – needs to be had, only this time without the restraints of having to preserve the fabric of the building at all costs. Ultimately, all decisions over the fabric of the local church, listed or not, would have to be jointly made and although legal responsibility for the church will have passed to the minster college, this should not mean responsibility remains solely with the college, let alone if the college does not have sole rights. As Graham Cray, Bishop of Maidstone, has said, 'at some time in the next decade a very serious re-negotiation with the nation has to take place'.[59]

'Local' ministry

The last piece of the jigsaw is the nature of the local ministry. What, if the minster church can provide all these multifarious services, should the local congregation be doing?

The exact answer will, once again, vary according to locality. The general guideline would be for the local congregation to be more self-governing than most parish churches presently are. They would see themselves more in the model of cell groups or clusters of cell groups than as current parish churches. They would offer the support, guidance and practical help that are key to fellowship and at the heart of any congregation, no matter what its size. This is not to say that they would be independent of ordained pastors, however, as they would work in close partnership with the relevant minister(s) from the minster church.

They would, nevertheless, have greater freedom than at present to shape the life and plans of the local congregation, drawing on the advice, support, guidance and encouragement available from the minster church. In the same way as villagers once attended minster churches while also being educated, pastored and helped by clergy, without ever being governed by them, modern-day local congregations would not only be involved in running and staffing their modern minster church but would also act as a separate local congregation, supported, equipped, guided and helped by the minster staff.

Problems and Potential

This, then, is an outline of what the minster model might look like. The obvious vagueness is necessitated by the system's necessary flexibility and local autonomy. The minster system has potential throughout England but may end up looking very different in Whitechapel and in Whitby.

As already observed, ecumenism is the key area ignored completely in this discussion. A thorough re-examination of the parish system in the minster light should provide many opportunities for fostering ecumenical links – for example, one of today's best known quasi-minster churches, St Thomas' Crookes, is a united Anglican and Baptist LEP – but these have been bypassed here in order to keep discussion of an already complex transition relatively simple. In much the same way, although theological considerations have underpinned many of the recommendations within the book, a more detailed and more explicit theological analysis is still needed.

Problems within the transition will be inevitable because it will involve genuinely tough decisions and because some people will obstruct it for wholly personal motives. The outline above will meet with as much irritation, and even anger, as agreement and enthusiasm.

Such difference of opinion is only to be expected but whatever else is arguable, the need for change is not. The present parish system is in many ways either inappropriate or actively harmful and demands reconsideration. Having been originally an arbitrary, 'secular' and flexible system, it has petrified over the years with sometimes dire effects. We are sentimental about it at our cost. As Leslie Paul wrote towards the end of his report, 'the organisation is not the end, but the spiritual function of the Church in the ministering of the sacraments and the preaching of the gospel is. If the organisation impedes this function, it ought to go.'

A.C. Smith, the pioneer of the South Ormsby experiment, wrote in his book on the project, 'what the church needs most of all is devotion rather than efficiency'.[60] He was, of course, right. No amount of strategic re-evaluation will transform the Church of England without faith, love, hope and prayer. But, in the company of these, it is time to rethink the English parish and to consider seriously how its future might lie in the long-dormant Anglo-Saxon minster system. We need to go back for the future.

Notes

1. Simon Jenkins, *England's Thousand Best Churches* (Harmondsworth: Penguin, 1999), xxx–xxxi.
2. Jenkins, *England's Thousand Best Churches*.
3. William of Malmesbury, *Life of Saint Wulfstan* (tr. J.H.F. Peile; Lampeter: Llanerch Press, 1996).
4. Thomas Wilson, *The State of England Anno Dom 1600* (ed. F.J. Fisher; 3rd series, vol. 16; London: Offices of the Society, 1936).
5. Nicholas Pounds, *The History of the English Parish* (Cambridge: Cambridge University Press, 2000), 49.
6. Pounds, *History of the English Parish*, 82.
7. *Visitation Articles and Injunctions of the Period of the Reformation* (ed. W.M. Frere & W.M. Kennedy; 1908–10) quoted in Eamon Duffy, *The Stripping of the Altars. Traditional Religion in England c.1400–c.1580* (London: Yale University Press, 1992), 480.
8. Rev James Tyalor quoted in Richard Morris, *Churches in this Landscape* (London: Phoenix, 1997), 438.
9. Flora Thompson, *Lark Rise to Candleford* (Oxford: OUP, 1939), 212.
10. Anon., *The Position of the Agricultural Labourer in the Past and in the Future* (1885), 43, quoted in Owen Chadwick, *The*

Victorian Church Vol. II (2 Vols; London: A. & C. Black, 1970), 156.

[11] W.K. Lowther-Clarke, *Facing the Facts or an Englishman's Religion* (London: James Nisbet, 1911).

[12] D.S. Cairns (ed.), *The Army and Religion* (London: Macmillan, 1919) quoted in Robin Gill, *The Empty Church Revisited* (London: SPCK, 2003).

[13] Ibid.

[14] Ibid.

[15] Ibid.

[16] Ibid.

[17] *Crockford's Clerical Dictionary 1927*, quoted in Roger Lloyd, *The Church of England 1900-1965* (London: SCM, 1966).

[18] Paul A. Welsby, *A History of the Church of England 1945–1980* (Oxford: Oxford University Press, 1984), 36.

[19] Ibid., 34.

[20] *Puzzled People. A Study in Popular Attitudes to Religion, Ethics, Progress and Politics in a London Borough. Prepared for the Ethical Union by Mass Observation* (London: Victor Gollancz, 1947). For more details on Mass Observation reports visit < www.sussex.ac.uk/library/massobs >.

[21] *Crockford's Clerical Dictionary 1955*, quoted in Lloyd, *The Church of England 1900-1965*.

[22] Welsby, *A History of the Church of England 1945–1980*, 39.

[23] Nick Spencer, *Beyond Belief?* (London Institute for Contemporary Christianity, 2003).

[24] Bob Jackson, *Hope for the Church* (London: Church House Publishing, 2002).

[25] Gill, *The Empty Church Revisited*.

[26] James Campbell, *The Anglo-Saxons* (Harmondsworth: Penguin, 1991).

[27] Bede, 'Letter to Egbert', in *English Historical Documents*, Vol. 1.

[28] Bede, *The Ecclesiastical History of the English People* (Harmondsworth: Penguin, 1990).

29 Bede, 'Letter to Egbert'.
30 John Blair and Richard Sharpe (eds.), *Pastoral Care Before the Parish* (Leicester: Leicester University Press, 1992), 277.
31 Ibid., 284.
32 Ibid., 284.
33 Ibid., 280.
34 Quoted in John Godfrey, *The English Parish* (London: SPCK, 1969), 27.
35 Bede, *Ecclesiastical History*.
36 Ibid.
37 Blair and Sharpe (eds.), *Pastoral Care*, 61.
38 Bede, *Ecclesiastical History*.
39 Campbell, *Anglo-Saxons*, 88.
40 Quoted in Blair and Sharpe (eds.), *Pastoral Care*, 9.
41 Ibid.
42 Thompson, *Lark Rise to Candleford*.
43 Edward Bellamy, *Looking Backward 2000–1987* (Ticker & Co., 1888).
44 Ibid.
45 Wladyslaw Reymont, *Peasants* (4 Vols.; tr. M.H. Dziewicki; Jarrolds: London, 1925-26) quoted in Pounds, *History of the English Parish*.
46 *Analysis*, Radio 4, *A Church that Matters*, first broadcast 21 November 2002.
47 Anon., *The Organisation of the Church in Large Centres of Population, with special Reference to the Church in St Pancras*, London (1900), quoted in Lloyd, *The Church of England 1900-1965*.
48 A.C. Smith, *The South Ormsby Experiment* (London: SPCK, 1960), 10.
49 A. Tindal Hart, 'Parson and Parish', in *Church and Countryside* (1958).
50 Leslie Paul, *The Deployment and Payment of the Clergy* (Church Information Office, 1964).
51 Welsby, *A History of the Church of England 1945–1980*.

52 *Church of England Newspaper* 17 January 1964, quoted in Welsby, *A History of the Church of England 1945-1980*, 134.

53 John Tiller, *A Strategy for the Church's Ministry* (London: CIO Publishing, 1983), 124.

54 Ibid.

55 Michale Paget-Wilkes, *Poverty, Revolution and the Church* (Exeter: Paternoster, 1981), 101.

56 Group and team ministries are different in practical (and legal) ways. A group ministry consists of two or more parsons who cooperate but are still beneficed incumbents, with all the rights and authorities that involves. A team ministry has only one beneficed priest, who is given the title rector and is the official incumbent of the (formerly separate) parishes. He or she shares the cure of souls with other full-time and stipendiary clergy, who are called 'team vicars' and who have 'incumbent status' i.e. security of tenure for the period of the pastoral scheme. Non-stipendiary ministers and lay ministers are also part of the team.

57 *Scottish Church Initiative for Union, Interim Report*, sec. 5.2.2.

58 Anthea Jones, *A Thousand Years of the English Parish: Medieval Patterns & Modern Interpretations* (Moreton-in-Marsh: Windrush, 2000).

59 Analysis, *A Church that Matters*.

60 Smith, *South Ormsby Experiment*, 87.